Love Beneath The Veil

JACQUELINE PITCHAL

LOVE BENEATH THE VEIL

Novel

Victoria

"Will my prince be here soon, *maman*?"

"Yes, darling, he won't be long now."

Sylvie gazed tenderly at her small daughter, Victoria, who was waiting impatiently for the arrival of her brother, her senior by nine years. She lived alone in Paris with her two children. Her husband had left her for a twenty-four year old. It had come as a massive shock. But what could she do? You can't hold a man back when the devil is dragging him towards another fate. She had cried and suffered, but out of her love for her two children, she'd survived. With the alimony her husband sent her and her profession as an architect, she wasn't doing too badly. Intelligent, distinguished, refined, and full of charm, she'd attracted her share of men, but having been burnt once she'd become more demanding as far as any new adventures were concerned and had turned all suitors away. Until now, she had failed to find any man who could replace her husband.

"But what can my prince be doing?!" the little girl asked petulantly.

The bell rang, followed by the sound of the key in the door. Victoria dashed into her brother's arms.

"I've been waiting for you a whole hour! You took an awfully long time coming here!"

Alexandre smiled. He set down his school bag and took Victoria into his arms to cover her with kisses. He had a protective side towards his little sister. Sylvie was overjoyed to see that her children got along so well together. Cécile, her little Caribbean maid, adored them, too, and took good care of the apartment, where harmony reigned. Victoria was an easy child to bring up. She was gay, lively, flirtatious, and charming. With her long, curly chestnut hair, her porcelain complexion, and her big aquamarine eyes, she was aware of her appeal and her ability to win over all those around her. Romantic by nature, she adored making up stories. Whenever she did happen to sulk, Alexandre would go to her in her room, always finding the right words to console her. Sniffling, she had confided to him, "When I grow up, I want to marry you!"

"But, princess, that's not possible, we're brother and sister!"

"Even so, we'll get married! Tonight, I want to sleep with you. I'm scared to fall asleep by myself. I always see a witch, dressed in black. She's small and ugly, with cruel eyes, and she wants to take you away from me. But in your arms, I won't be afraid anymore. You'll tell me beautiful stories."

"What are you thinking about?"

Victoria gave a start. Pierre's voice had brought her back to the present. He'd joined her for the weekend at the Hassler Villa Medici Hotel in Rome, because she had to do some photos for a magazine. Her job as a fashion model involved traveling all over the world. That delighted her. She adored Rome, which exuded an unreal beauty. How could one be indifferent to this city, the head and the memory of the entire world, where over twenty centuries of history swarmed all over its hills? She had discovered ancient Rome, with the Forum, the true heart of its social life; the Palatine hill, where Roman civilization was born; the Coliseum, where mock naval battles and gladiator fights had been held; and

Renaissance Rome, with the Vatican and its famous museums... She loved to go strolling along the Tiber, have coffee at the Café Greco on the Via dei Condotti, the meeting-place of poets and musicians during the previous century, and walk from St. Peter's Basilica to the Sistine Chapel, with Michelangelo's admirable frescoes. From the Piazza Navona to the bell-towers of Sant'Agnese, Rome was radiant! She remained the fabled city with over two thousand years of history and inexhaustible treasures. So much beauty overwhelmed her soul.

Pierre, her friend, was thirty-three years old. A lawyer, his career did not allow him to accompany Victoria in all her travels. But madly in love with him, she was living out a romance novel. He was passionate, delicate, loving, and thoughtful. The ideal man. She was aware how lucky she was. He also had an attractive physique: brown hair with green eyes, average height, and a charmer, he knew how to talk to women, seduce them with his intelligence, his culture, and his *savoir-faire*.

Pierre drew her out of her thoughts. "Something worrying you?"

"I was thinking about my brother. It's the first time he's forgotten to phone me and wish me a happy birthday, especially since we were born on the same day, although not the same year!"

"He doesn't know you're in Rome. And he does have his own life, his own activities..."

"You're right, of course. But my brother means everything to me. I really do miss him."

"Thanks a lot!"

"Oh! Forgive me, my love. But with you, it's not the same thing;"

The telephone rang, and she picked up. The hotel concierge announced that flowers were being sent up. When the knock came at the door, Victoria went to open it. Pierre went pale at the sight of two enormous bouquets of flowers. She unfastened the greeting cards. One was from Pierre, but the other from her brother. And the composition of Alexandre's bouquet was clearly superior. "Always the blunderer," Victoria thought to herself. Pierre gritted his teeth to stop himself from making an angry comment. There were many times when he had a mad urge to smash Alexandre's face in, but he controlled himself for Victoria's sake. At the slightest remark concerning her brother, she leapt like a panther. She had no other family but him in the world. For her, he was a god. Their father had died of throat cancer at the age of forty-three. Seven months later, their mother, who had just celebrated her fortieth birthday, had a serious car accident, dying on the spot. These successive shocks had brought the two siblings even closer together. They had a loving affection for one another. Fortunately, he was only her brother! Especially since he had everything: he was intelligent, seductive, cultivated, generous, and witty.

Pierre was very much in love with Victoria, it had taken great effort to win her heart.

"Oh, my love, you've spoiled me. Your flowers are superb."

"Your brother has..."

"My brother is crazy. He always has to mark his territory. For him, it's automatic, from you, it's full of love..." she said, enfolding herself in his arms.

Pierre was the opposite of Alexandre, both mentally and physically. Alexandre was twenty-seven years old, and strikingly handsome. A mix of romanticism and virility, he was big, with brown hair and penetrating, velvety black eyes, as well as an athlete's body. She liked his bold temperament and his intelligence combined with vigor, endurance, good humor, and generosity. The only fault she could find with him was that he was too egocentric when it came to women, except for her. He had a good job as a manager for a foreign bank.

Pierre was aware that Victoria could slip away from him like a cat. She was feline, independent, unpredictable, mysterious, and dreamy. But she purred in his arms, and made him melt. She was an enchantress. Although she let him think that he commanded, it was she who guided his heart.

Victoria's cell phone rang in the bedroom. When she answered it, her face lit up.

"Alex! You remembered our birthday? You crazy guy! Where are you? In London? What! That can't be true, I must be dreaming!

She turned toward Pierre.

"It's Alex, he's in the hotel lobby!"

She spoke again to her brother. "Come right up! We're in room 712."

Victoria was quivering just like a little girl, her cheeks pink with happiness. Pierre felt like he was about to explode. It was he who had told Alexandre that they were in Rome. But Pierre had only wanted him to call as a surprise for Victoria's. But now this completely ruined his plan for a lovers' weekend alone together. Alexandre arrived, in superb form, a brilliant smile lighting up his face. He gave Pierre a pat on the back, and kissed his sister. He ordered champagne and *petits fours*.

"My little sister's eighteenth birthday, that calls for a

drink," he said, clinking glasses with them.

Victoria was in heaven. When her brother was there, it was like a whirlwind. He made the stars move for her.

"This evening, we're going to party. You are my guests. Victoria, invite your girlfriends to come clubbing with us, around midnight at Jacky O's. I have friends in Rome, too, I'll give them a ring. After all, it's not everyday you turn eighteen!"

Alex noticed that Pierre was looking a bit put out.

"Don't worry, old man. I'm stealing her away from you this evening, but I'll return her to you later tonight."

"Did you bring a girlfriend with you?" Victoria inquired.

"A girlfriend? You can't stand any of them, especially on our birthdays! I came on my own, just for you, princess."

Alexander took both of them to dinner at a trendy restaurant, where people came to be seen and to see celebrities. The decor was romantic, with a ravishing, flowered terrace. The customers stopped at tables to greet one another. It was a fashionable place, where friends shared the same tastes and the same pleasures. Italian accents sang out loudly, and laughter burst forth. Things were in full swing, and everyone was relaxed and happy. The mouth-watering odor of tomato sauce seasoned with basil tickled noses and stimulated appetites. The waiter had saved them a round table situated so that could they could observe the entire room. Surrounded by her boyfriend and her brother, Victoria's face radiated joy. She couldn't help nibbling at a *grissini*. Her brother gazed at her tenderly, admiring her queenly bearing. He was glad that she had kept her long chestnut hair with auburn highlights, framing her Madonna-like face. She had immense, almond-shaped eyes of an indefinable blue that changed with the weather, an aquiline nose, and a sensual, slightly pouting mouth that made her irresistible. He liked her gestures, her laughter, and her voice. In a word, he adored her! Victoria caught him looking at her and smiled back, her eyes shining like stars, sending him all the tenderness she felt for him. The waiter brought the three glasses of champagne that Alex had ordered for them.

"Happy birthday, little sister!" he said, clinking his glass with hers.

"Happy birthday to you, too."

"Happy birthday to both of you," Pierre chimed in, with a twinge in his heart.

Pierre would have much preferred to be alone with her. He was jealous of the tenderness and the complicity that flowed back and forth between them. But he was also ashamed of feeling this way, which was unworthy of him. Victoria lifted her napkin and was dumbfounded. There was a present lying there. As she opened the package, she began to worry: it had better not be from her brother! But she was reassured when she saw the bracelet with three rows of pearls that she had admired with Pierre in the window display of a jeweler in Paris.

"Oh, Pierre, you shouldn't have!" she said, touched. "It's magnificent."

Pierre gallantly attached the bracelet about her wrist with loving fingers.

"I'm so spoiled. Thank you, my love," she said, kissing him warmly on the cheek.

Alexander felt awkward in the presence of the lovebirds, who obviously would have liked to have celebrated this moment *tête-à-tête*.

After their delicious dinner, they found themselves, as agreed, in a nightclub where the upper crust of Rome partied until dawn. Victoria had invited four of her colleagues, all of them fashion models like herself: Sarah, Nathalie, Fiona, and Priscia. Alexander had also invited friends of his, four superb Italians, slightly macho, their eyes sparkling with charm. The evening promised to be sizzling. After making introductions, her brother generously ordered champagne all round. The party got off to a smooth start, as people placed themselves, almost instinctively, according to their affinities. Couples soon formed... Laughter began to bubble forth. Victoria's friends were radiant. The men deployed their humor, their powers of seduction, and their *savoir-faire* with these beautiful, intelligent girls. When it came to serenading women no one equaled the Italians, with their hot blood and easy compliments... There was a general euphoria in the air. People came here to have fun, to live intensely for the moment. They drank, danced, sang, and laughed. On the dance-floor, they got rid of their worries, their heartaches, and their problems. The sound system boomed with the latest hits, so loudly that no one could hear themselves speak, but everyone was intoxicated with pleasure. The young male wolves hunted, and the girls cooed like doves.

Victoria stuck close to Pierre, knowing other women all too well: the minute you turned your back, they'd slip him their telephone number! She'd already spotted a pretty red-head who had been giving him the eye ever since they arrived. The fact that he was with Victoria only added to his success! Some women were excited by the idea of seducing a man who was already spoken for.

Victoria herself couldn't understand that sort of behavior. For her, a man who was accompanied by a woman was automatically sexless in her eyes. It even repelled her! But to each their own taste. Alex, after asking Pierre's permission, invited her to dance. But once they arrived on the dance-floor, the music had changed to a slow tune. They looked at one another, hesitantly.

"Will you give me this dance?", he asked her, in a slightly mocking manner.

"Why not?" she replied, adopting the same tone. "There's no danger of me falling for you."

Alex put his arms around her and pressed her tenderly against him. She smelled his scent, felt his cheek rubbing hers, and his arm gripping her waist. The languorous music made her heart beat faster, especially when Alex hugged her more closely. She couldn't help thinking that the woman he married would be very lucky indeed. All her woman friends looked at him with desire, but Alex remained indifferent to their charms. That was the reason he'd invited his friends that evening. He was inaccessible and unpredictable, making his own choices. He didn't like other people imposing things upon him, and was a very hard nut to crack. Didn't they say that men were like shadows: if you follow them, they flee, and if you flee, they follow? Even with his sister, he was playing the game of seduction during this slow dance.

The music stopped. He pressed his head against her cheek in order to murmur in her ear. "You are more and more attractive, the most beautiful woman here this evening. If you weren't my adorable little sister, I'd try to pick you up myself. Come on, I have a present for you."

He drew her apart from the crowd, away from Pierre, to a corner protected from prying eyes. The music had gone back to a frenzied dance beat. From his jacket pocket, Alex produced a little box. She opened it, and was stupefied by the royal gift inside. It was a double ring set with precious stones, which joined between two small diamond hearts, the kind called "You and Me".

"It's sublime!"

"There's nothing too beautiful for you, princess. I saw this ring in the window, and I said to myself that it would suit my little doll of a sister. I couldn't resist the pleasure of offering it to you for our birthday. You should put it on your right hand, since the left is reserved for your engagement ring. That way, you'll think of me."

"But I don't need a ring to think of you!" she cried as she slipped the ring onto her finger.

She held out her right hand, blushing with emotion, to admire the beauty of the piece of jewelry.

"Don't wear it this evening. Pierre wouldn't like it. He's so jealous – I can see why. Tell him that it belonged to *maman*. Sometimes you need to know when to lie."

Victoria was moved: she was incredibly lucky to have such a dream of a brother. She wrapped her arms tenderly around his neck, giving him a kiss as thanks. Regretfully, she took the ring off her finger and placed it back in the box, which she slipped into her purse.

The partying finished up at dawn. Both Pierre and Alex had arranged things well, so that Victoria would keep an unforgettable memory of her eighteenth birthday. But it was in the arms of her lover that she received the most wonderful gift in the world.

Upon returning to Paris, she was caught up in the whirlwind of activity. Her parents had insisted that she pass her high school examinations before launching herself on a career in fashion. But once she had her diploma, she had presented herself to a big modeling agency in order to fulfill her life's dream and had been lucky enough to be accepted. She crisscrossed the entire world, staying at the finest hotels and traveling by Concorde. The work itself demanded sacrifices, and required being available at all times. Her private life came second, or even third. It was difficult to face the loneliness of a hotel room when an ardent lover was waiting for you on the other side of the world. She was afraid that Pierre would grow tired of this situation. Often, she called him up around two o'clock in the morning: his telephone rang and rang or the answering machine told her to leave a message. Pierre had lots of success with women, that much was obvious. He must run into plenty of temptations. Victoria didn't dare ask too many questions. Life is a choice, and it was she, and she alone, who would plot her destiny and figure out which direction she wanted to go. Her ambition was to become a top model. Her fairy godmothers had leaned over her cradle to give her the body that would allow her to devote herself to this work she so loved.

In the shadows, her brother was always there for her. She had her own life, and he had his. He was very discreet. In contrast, his girlfriends weren't discreet at all. They all came to sob on her shoulder. As they told it, he was a torturer! Her brother was a Don Juan, who seduced them and then fled. Could it be he had too many choices? She herself wouldn't like to be in love with the kind of seducer who made women suffer. You would have to be a masochist to put up with the way he treated them: the infidelities, the ridicule, the humiliation, the suffering! All for a few hours of pleasure! Despite themselves, they slipped into love's trap. Until now, he'd never made any woman happy, as Victoria herself had pointed out to him on occasion. His girlfriends were superb, intelligent, and ready to do anything for him. It was too bad he was unable to settle down with one of them. But why worry herself over her brother's life? After all, it was up to him to make up his own mind!

Betrayal

Victoria gave a start when the alarm clock went off. She had trouble rousing herself from her slumber. She was supposed to leave for Tunisia to take part in a fashion show being held in the middle of the desert. While running her bath, she prepared her breakfast: Marco Polo tea, whose perfumed, sensual aroma she adored, a spoonful of honey, and freshly squeezed orange juice. She couldn't have anything else if she wanted to stay slim. Her job did not allow her any leeway. She felt anxious, although there was no reason for it. Since the death of her parents, and particularly the loss of her mother, she'd been troubled. She felt amputated from a part of herself, there was a horrible emptiness, a gaping hole, something missing within her. Her mother had bestowed all the love in the world upon her. She had done everything in her power to see that her two children grew up in the comfort of a privileged milieu.

Victoria had kept her mother's apartment in a handsome old building of dressed stone. It was luminous, with a balcony – that she had attentively planted with flowers – overlooking a square. In the springtime, she enjoyed the birds' songs, the superb garden, and the magnificent trees. Alex and she had grown up here. She did not want to move, wishing to preserve the atmosphere of the past, while removing some mementos that she found too painful. Her mother's room had been transformed completely, including the furniture. The sight of the room as it used to be had been unbearable to her, evoking her mother's presence constantly. Now it was reserved for the use of her friends. The apartment was furnished with a mixture of antiques and modern pieces. In the living room, facing the fireplace, there was an immense sofa with cushions and two matching armchairs, upholstered in beige with tiny flowers, which provided a very warm, cozy touch. It was pleasant to curl up in the sofa, put on some music, read, or daydream in front of the fire. She spent long moments looking at the flames licking the logs, listening to the crackling wood that gave off an intoxicating scent, feeling the sense of well-being and sweet warmth that spread throughout the apartment. She was always fascinated by this spectacle.

Victoria had a preference for antique furniture, objects, and paintings. They had a life, a history, a past of their own. When she had free time, she loved to go hunting in the flea markets or the auction rooms. It was one of her favorite pastimes. Her mother had given her a taste for painting, for sculpture, and for beautiful things. "Art nourishes the soul", she had told her daughter. Victoria looked at her mother's photo fondly, caressing the frame which sat on the dresser in the bedroom, then brought it to her lips. Tears ran down her face. They had always got on well together, the two of them. Her mother had been so sweet, although she possessed a strong personality. Victoria shook off her sadness. Her mother lived on in her heart.

At the airport, she located her travel group. There was a problem with the reservations and the trip was canceled. She came back home and allowed herself a lazy day. Pierre had told her yesterday that he had a busy schedule and that he would be dining at home. She would stop by her delicatessen that evening to pick up some cooked dishes for him. A little surprise dinner for her lover. She was sure he'd like that.

It was already after eight when she arrived in front of his building. There was nowhere to park! After circling several times, she was finally obliged to find a place further away. She was maneuvering into it when in the rear-view mirror she spied Pierre's flashy Porsche coming out of the garage. Out of a reflex, she ducked down. The car passed and she sat back up. Pierre wasn't alone: a young blonde was cuddled up next to him. She tilted her head and he gave her a kiss. Victoria felt herself growing faint. She nevertheless reacted and decided to follow the car. Pierre was too preoccupied to think of looking in his rear-view mirror. He suspected nothing: Victoria was supposed to be in Tunisia. Her heart leapt in her chest and she had trouble breathing. Sweat pearled her brow. He drove towards the Rue du Faubourg-Saint-Honoré and stopped in front of the Hôtel Coste. The swine! He was taking this other woman to dinner at one of her favorite restaurants. What a boor! She felt ill, as if she was going to be sick. The bellboy took the car, and the entwined couple went inside. What should she do? She wasn't about to enter the place, frequented by high Parisian society, to make a scene and cover herself in ridicule. He could at least have gone somewhere more discreet. Here, everyone, or almost, knew one another. Alex came here regularly. Tilting her head back, she sat there lost in her furious thoughts. Tears stung her eyes. She shivered.

"Aren't you feeling well, *mademoiselle*?"

She opened her eyes, ashamed of having lost control herself for a few seconds. The bellboy was looking at her, slightly worried.

"No, no, it's nothing. Thank you."

She started the engine, and drove around Paris aimlessly. She was hurt. She had thought that Pierre truly loved her, that it was serious between them. That morning, before her departure, she'd called him from her cell phone.

"I'll miss you, my love. This evening, I'm going to stay home quietly and update some of my files," he'd told her.

What a liar! It was only because of the mix-up with the reservations that the dream had been broken. It must not have been the first time. How could she have been so naive! It was wishful thinking to believe that a man could be faithful. Yet, some of them must be, surely? Was her constant traveling to blame?

How foolish of her to think that her body was irreplaceable! Everything was muddled in her head. Suddenly, she remembered that she had lent her apartment to her brother, who was passing through Paris. His own apartment was undergoing some repairs. He was supposed to be arriving around eight o'clock. She hoped he wasn't with a girlfriend. She would ask him to take her to dinner at Coste's and surprise Pierre there. With this idea in mind, she calmed herself a little. She would make herself very beautiful. Pierre was in for a shock! She was already wondering what attitude he would take towards her. When she arrived in front her building she saw the lights were on in her apartment. Perhaps Alex was not alone. She would have to be discreet. She slipped her key in the lock: the lights were on in the living room and there was music playing. Apparently, Alex was in the guest room. She went into her own bedroom, dropped her bag, and was taking off her coat when she heard the voice of a man who wasn't her brother. Surprised, she quietly opened the door a fraction. She was petrified by what she saw. There was a handsome man in the nude, with a glass of whiskey in his hand!

"Alexandre, do you want me to pour you a glass?"

"Yes, please," replied her brother, coming into the living room, dressed only in his underwear and a shirt that he was buttoning.

She turned off the light in her bedroom to avoid drawing their attention. She was shaking uncontrollably. No, it wasn't possible! She lay down upon her bed in order not to faint. It wasn't the end of the world, but she'd been so proud of his virility and the macho, protective side of his nature. She had plenty of homosexual friends whom she liked, but to think that her brother was one of them! Her Alex, her very own prince! She'd been jealous of his girlfriends, but his being with a man was even worse! In short, she was the unhappiest woman on earth, to the point of forgetting all about Pierre and his beautiful blonde. She was angry at Alex for having brought this handsome hunk back to her place. To be sure, he could not have foreseen her unexpected return. But how inconsiderate of him. What was it that drew them together? There were more and more of them these days, the handsomest men were rarely heterosexual. There must be something about women that put them off. The competition was formidable! Women would have to become aware that there was a problem, that they needed to call themselves into question and make more of an effort at being seductive.

The two men were still in the living room. She got up

and put her ear to the door to overhear their conversation.

She heard her brother's friend ask, "Where do you want to have dinner?"

"I have no idea."

It would be the final straw, Victoria thought, if they went to Coste's, too!

"How about the Italian restaurant?"

"Excellent idea!"

Victoria did not dare move in the darkness. She remained still for several long minutes until they left the apartment. She shook with sobs. God, she felt bad! She didn't know if it was mainly because of Pierre or because of her brother. She went to the bathroom and looked at herself in the mirror. She was unrecognizable, as if she had applied a mask to her face. She knew there were lots of men with repressed desires in that particular direction, but who didn't dare act on them. One would be astonished by just how many, if their secret fantasies could be detected. Perhaps even Pierre? And now here she was believing that all men were homosexuals, on the pretext that her brother was one! If he made women suffer so, it was because he didn't like them. She had found the secret flaw and she had a dizzying sensation of falling from a great height. What an evening! She had wanted to surprise Pierre by dropping in on him unexpectedly. Now she knew what the word "surprise" could hide. There was no longer any question of sleeping at her place. They would be coming back from the restaurant. At that idea, she grew pale. She remembered that she'd left the packages from the delicatessen in her car. What should she do with them? With a little luck, her brother hadn't had time to open the refrigerator. He would think that she'd left them especially for him. So much the better. She'd have to find a hotel for the next four days. No, she had a better idea: she would go to the airport and pick a destination from the departure board. Rome? Madrid? After receiving these shocks, Paris was simply too suffocating for her. She needed a breath of fresh air.

At the airport she hurried over to the ticket counter. The flight to Rome was announced and there were still seats. She punched a friend's number on her cell phone. David answered, he was in a restaurant.
"Victoria! Where are you?"
"At the Paris airport. I'm taking a flight to spend four days in Rome."
David's cheerful voice resounded in the receiver, "Great! Come and sleep at my house, there's no question of you staying at a hotel."
"But..."
"That's an order! Humor me. What time do you arrive?"
"11:30 p.m."
"Perfect, my chauffeur will pick you up. *Ciao, ciao, amore!* See you in a bit."
Wonderful David, if he only knew. But no one would ever know. On the plane, she had stomach cramps and difficulty breathing. She asked for champagne to give herself courage and face the cruel truth. It was strange, she was more disappointed with her brother than by Pierre's behavior. Alex was hers, her own flesh and blood. As if he belonged to her, was inside of her. How would she behave towards him from now on? He would be distressed, mortally wounded, if he knew that she had found him out. His attitude towards her would change. She would have to let events settle, let time do its work.

At eighteen, she knew nothing of love and still had everything to learn about the effects, the forces, and the currents that it unleashed, ravaging everything in its path. Love was untamable. It released passions, raised you to ecstasy, and then left you without illusions. Love was alchemy.

David was considerate enough to come to the airport to pick her up, accompanied by two of his friends. His exuberance, good humor, his gestures, his Italian accent, and excellent French all made her forget her sorrow for a few instants. She wanted to put on a happy face, even though she was wounded inside.

"Victoria!" he cried upon seeing her. "You're looking radiant, how lovely to see you! I adore it when you surprise me like this," he said, kissing her.

He introduced her to his friends.

"She's beautiful, isn't she? I wasn't lying to you. She is the most sensual fashion model around, my Victoria. The woman of my dreams."

Victoria had trouble sleeping that night, haunted by nightmares. She dreamt she saw her brother embracing a man, who turned out to be none other than Pierre!

David, who was both intuitive and discreet, organized a heavenly stay for her in the city, so that she would forget her sorrows. Discovering Rome in his company was a perpetual enchantment. He was a fantastic guide. Introducing her to Baroque art, he spoke of its mysteries. "From 1580 to 1620, the craze for building took hold of the Popes. In the space of two generations, the Eternal City was utterly transformed. The architect Bernini was at work everywhere. That's how we got all these expressive statues that turn the stones and the water of our squares into their stage. Then there was Borromini, whose vision of the world was more secret and internal, mixing dreams with the search for the divine. He built two marvelous chapels: one dedicated to the Three Kings and the other to Sant'Ivo. These two architects and sculptors lived in the same period and were great... enemies."

He showed her the Campo dei Fiori, with its enormous market occupying an immense rectangular square. Fruits, vegetables, and flowers over-spilled from the stands. It was picturesque, and Italian voices sang out everywhere, a joyful clamor orchestrating the heart of Rome. On Via Giulia, craftsmen and small shopkeepers bustled about in the shadows at the feet of palaces and churches, as if they had not stopped working there since the 15th century. He took her behind the Piazza Navona, where the lively heart of working-class Rome still beat in the Parioni and Ponte neighborhoods. The ground floors of the old houses were full of artisans' workshops. There one could shop for furniture, objets d'art, and old prints. There were *trattorias* full of charm. Victoria, with her romantic inclinations, wanted to visit the gardens of Adonis on the Palatine hill, where history joined myth, each stone and plant hiding a legend. It was a place for contemplation.

"They say," David confided to her, "that for centuries the Palatine hill has had a mysterious power. Like a breeze that takes the hand of visitors..."

Its gardens revealed their mysteries, at the core of which lay a vineyard. It had belonged to the Barberini family up until 1911, whose traces could still be seen among the thriving fig trees and the tall weeds of ancient forums. But beneath the vineyard was the first step into the mystery: a temple. This temple had been built by Héliogabalus, the cruel Sun-worshipping emperor who had martyred Saint Sebastian. Archeological digs had established that Antinoius, the boy loved by the emperor Hadrian had been buried in this sacred place. His tomb, which had been moved after the emperor's death, proved that the Barberini vineyard were situated on the very site of the famous gardens of Adonis, mentioned in ancient texts...

David was a cultivated, intelligent man who was passionate about art. A man of refined tastes with a big heart. Victoria was lucky to know him. He was an antique dealer, whose business was flourishing. He had a magnificent apartment with a terrace in a residential neighborhood. In the morning, they had breakfast together. It was an intimate moment that lent itself to confiding matters. David was already elegant, wearing his dark-red dressing gown. They chatted between two cups of tea with toast.

"I've worked hard since the age of fourteen. I'm a self-made man. I owe my success to my own efforts... and to luck. 'Ask heaven for a good harvest, and continue to sow.' That's a Slovene saying that has often comforted me in hard times."

He forgot to say that his audacity had also played a part. His character had shaped his destiny.

"At forty, I'll stop working in this trade. I've already arrived at the height of my career. I can't go any higher. I want to do something else, just to please myself."

His mixed Lebanese, Jewish, and Italian origins gave him an Eastern air. He received his friends in a lordly manner, but without pretension. He was very selective in his relations. His taste for living, for parties, for beautiful things, and his Italian accent all added to his charm. Medium in height, with brown hair, he wore tinted glasses that hid the color of his eyes. His face was pleasant and friendly. His personality sparkled like champagne. He was sentimental, but tough in business matters. His dream was to become a movie actor. He wanted to sell up everything to go into cinema! Victoria, without contradicting him, suggested that he make a small trial run before committing himself fully. She was going to introduce him to a friend who worked in films. She believed in him, he had the talent to become a comic actor. He was a natural, she was sure that he would succeed without running the risk of losing his fortune. She had met him the year before at the Cannes film festival one evening. He was surrounded by sharks who'd marked him as a tempting prey and would not let go of him for even a single second. But they didn't know David. When a man as young as he was achieved success, he wasn't likely to let himself be misled. Only love could make intelligent, powerful people become crazy, blind, and vulnerable. David shared her table during a gala dinner. They'd immediately connected and exchanged addresses.

"I sense you are feeling melancholy, Victoria. Your eyes are drowning in sadness. Is there a problem?"
"No, no, everything's going marvelously well. I'm touched by your hospitality and your kindness. I'm happy to be in Rome, I feel good here. I'm nourished by its splendors."
He spelled out the day's program to her:
"We'll go see Gian-Marco, a childhood friend of mine who's a sculptor. He has a superb house just outside of

Rome. He adores receiving visitors and cooking meals for friends. At his place, we'll meet some fascinating people. You'll enjoy it, I'm sure. We'll return about 6 p.m., because I'm taking you to a gallery showing. I promised to stop by with you. Then there's a party at Guido's"

During their journey, Victoria admired the Roman countryside, very lush with forests of olive trees... Her eyes were refreshed by all this greenery that stretched to the horizon. In the distance, small villages huddled against the hills. All this beauty was breathtaking. They passed through one village just before arriving at Gian-Marco's. Little old men with caps on their heads conversed on benches in the main square, shaded by plane trees. Others were playing *petanca*.

When they got to their destination, Gian-Marco greeted them with open arms and introduced his friends. The day turned warm and friendly. Their host insisted that they stay for dinner, but they couldn't accept.

Victoria was caught up in a whirlwind. It seemed like David was trying to make her head spin during these four days, taking her to lunches, gallery showings, cocktails, parties, trendy clubs... Victoria collapsed into bed at four in the morning, exhausted, not having had time to think or even to do any shopping. Her stay in Rome went by in the blink of an eye.

On the plane that took her back to Paris, she thought about the attitude she would take concerning Pierre. Keeping calm was the wisest course. She had to master her feelings and not reveal anything. Concealment was the art of kings. But she was still young, so that this demanded a great deal of self-control. She would make him pay dearly for his behavior, however. But how? She didn't have a clue. Above all, no reproaches, that would only lead to ridiculing herself. She would derive strength from indifference, detachment, and contempt. She would tear free from her jealousy by a brutal breakup. If he insisted, she would tell him that she didn't love him anymore. In any case, he had destroyed her trust in him and things could never be the same as before. She would simply have to steel her nerve and cast him aside. There was an English proverb that said, "To make a good marriage, a husband should be deaf, and a wife should be blind." But she wasn't yet ready to adopt that kind of program. Later, perhaps, when the years had passed, and she no longer had a choice... For now, she would have to teach her pain to be proud, through total silence. But the hardest part still remained: taking action. Reason often becomes a shackle, preventing one from ever reaching any decision or taking that necessary leap. She still dreamed of love with a capital "L". Love for her was an ocean of life, something that would vibrate her entire being. She wanted to bathe in that ocean, dive into it, nourish herself with happiness, with ecstasy. Sadly, all that seemed like wishful thinking now.

But during these last four days in Rome, she'd been able to stand back and reassess. Now she felt ready to face the return.

Upon her arrival in Paris, she found a note from her brother, accompanied by white
orchids, thanking her for the loan of the apartment. She'd deliberately left her cell phone in Paris so she wouldn't be tempted to answer it. There were fifteen calls! She left a message at Pierre's home, when she

knew he'd be at his office:

"My love, I'm sorry, but I couldn't get through to your office. I'll call you when I can."

She had to stand fast in her resolve. She called her agency to see if there was work for her. Her agent said they were asking for her to do a shoot in Saint Barth. Departure was in forty-eight hours. She told the building *concierge* that she wasn't in for anyone. She blocked her telephone, after leaving a message for her brother so that he wouldn't worry about her silence. This departure was a welcome one. Pierre would wonder what was going on, especially since he must be feeling guilty. Before flying off to the islands, she would write him a short note breaking things off with him. She wanted to keep control of the situation. She would gather new strength and come back after soaking up some sunshine. The idea itself already lightened her mood.

But then she thought of her brother and her heart sank again. A strange feeling had gripped her since that evening, one she was unable to define, but nevertheless hurt her. She has never been able to tame her wild temperament. She was always walking a tight wire, threatened by a powerful, subterranean, unconscious reality fermenting deep inside her, that could erupt at any moment like a volcano. From time to time, she was submerged by a wave instinctive passion that she sensed could only lead to tragedy. When this happened, she became the prisoner of the fantasies of her inner universe. And her brother knew that.

The "corsair"

In Saint Barth, she was out of luck, the execrable weather did nothing at all to improve her mood. The sky was intensely black and the rain fell in big drops, leaving wide streaks on the windows. Then the heavens lit up with big lightning bolts; thunder boomed. The freezing wind howled a wild complaint that echoed in the distance. It struck with incredible violence. The storm aroused a raging sea that broke against the reefs, unrolling a carpet of white foam. At the edge of the beach, immense waves boiled furiously on the sand, rolling over pebbles, and then retreated suddenly, sucking everything along with them. Objects on the terrace were being smashed to bits. Nature was reeling dangerously... Chill penetrated under the doors, and Victoria shivered in her sweater.

"Are you cold?"

Victoria turned. The voice of the young man was warm and pleasant, his physique as well. He had brown hair and black eyes, a beautiful smile that revealed dazzling white teeth, brightening a tanned face that was dripping with rain. His hair, jeans, and boots, were all soaking wet!

"You're brave to be out in a storm like this!" Victoria replied, staring at him.

She thought he was very cute, a real corsair...

"I didn't have a choice," he answered in the same tone. "I had to help my friends anchor their boat safely. In this gale, it might have been carried out to sea. The sea can be the most imaginative, the most beautiful, and the most passionate of mistresses, offering unforgettable, unending pleasures... But then without warning it can become formidable and unpredictable, a traitoress like any woman..."

She looked at him, astonished by the comparison. She wanted to reply that men were worse, but restrained herself. The stranger continued:

"Did you just arrive?"

"Yes."

"You're unlucky. Yesterday the weather was magnificent. Let's hope this doesn't last long... Are you staying a few days with us?"

"Ten days."

"After tomorrow, it seems, the weather will improve. You'll be able to get a tan before returning to Paris. You do live in Paris, don't you?"

"Yes."

"I'm going upstairs to my room to get changed. We can have a drink together after, if you like."

"Why not?"

The young man started to leave, then turned back.

"I forgot to introduce myself. My name is Marco. And you?"

"Victoria."

"See you in awhile, Victoria."

Marco! A teasing smile appeared on Victoria's lips. Why not Marco Polo? Her very own corsair!

Victoria sat at a table with the other models working on the shoot, listening to them chatter. She tried to keep a relaxed face. Nadège, a ravishing Swedish girl, exclaimed:

"What a handsome boy!"

Victoria recognized her "corsair". The latter, unfazed by the group of beautiful girls, approached and went straight up to Victoria with a smile on his face. Casually, he took her by the hand.

"Will you ladies permit me to borrow her?"

She was surprised. Her friends looked at her with envy. The scene amused her. She found him attractive, a force seemed to emanate from him. He took her to a quiet corner, facing the sea, and ordered two glasses of champagne. She learned that he lived in New York and worked for a film production company. He liked sports: polo, tennis, golf, cricket, scuba diving, plus all the nautical disciplines. "New York," he explained, "is an exciting city, but stressful." He was interesting and cultivated. He had lived in the United States since he was a child, but had been born in Argentina. That's where he got his dark hair and smoldering eyes... From his behavior and his courteous gestures, she deduced that he was from a good family. He was a very virile, with a romantic touch. But Victoria's heart was not available, with Pierre's face still dancing before her eyes.

"Is this your first visit to Saint Barth?"

"Yes."

"You're going to like it here, it's a paradise, the inlets are like caskets of jewels, the beaches are superb, and the sea bottom is inexhaustible..."

She listened to him, observing his gestures, his way of expressing himself. He was very charming and was visibly trying hard to seduce her. But despite his winning ways, Victoria remained indifferent to him. He proposed that they dine together and spend the rest of the evening at a club. She thanked him for his invitation, but refused, inventing an excuse in order not to offend him. Being a gentleman, he didn't insist. He was familiar enough with women to realize that it was not worth pursuing this conversation right now: they weren't hitting it off. He liked Victoria, but her reticence made him uneasy. He wasn't used to meeting resistance and his pride was hurt. In general, he achieved his aims easily, even with the most inaccessible women.

But he'd misjudged Victoria. Her inner world was a thousand leagues from any familiar lands. At night, she often walked there in her dreams. During the daytime, she had an eagle's eye that stripped people in a single glance. The force of her youth and her animal instinct gave her the audacity to go beyond herself, encasing her bad memories behind glass so that they could not return to claw at her heart. The shock she had just suffered made her aware that nothing was permanent. She was not the first person to be disappointed in love. The Hindus say that one must always face one's karma. Destiny leaves no room for self-pity. People can never escape from divine justice or circumvent its consequences.

She wanted to be alone. She ordered dinner from room service. Outside, the storm still raged. The walls of her bedroom shuddered and lightning struck, the flashes illuminating the interior. She cast a glance outdoors, her eyes adapting to the surrounding shadows. Against the window panes she heard the rattling of sand thrown up by the violently howling wind. The sea was an immense black abyss in the middle of this menacing night. She shivered, dwelling on her sorrow, recalling the details of how she'd been betrayed. Her anxiety became tumultuous.

She resisted the urge to dial Pierre's number. She wanted to hear the sound of his voice. Before, that might have been possible, but these days things was different, numbers were displayed, revealing the identity of the caller. She didn't want him to know that she desired to hear him. She ended up falling into an uneasy sleep, disturbed by nightmares. Her dreams were marked by the echoes of her turmoil.

The silky sound of the sea and its salty breath brought her out of her slumber. She had breakfast on the terrace. The sky had grown peaceful following the bout of bad weather. She was dazzled by the almost unreal panorama, with the becalmed turquoise sea powdered by the golden sunshine stretching before her in its infinite sweetness. Despite the early hour, the sun's rays burned on her shoulders and face...

During her stay, she devoted herself to her work, which proved exhausting. Often waking at 5 a.m., her days were filled with photo sessions and advertising shoots that lasted long into the night ... She had little free time. But she adored this job. She liked working with Tony, a talented photographer. He knew how to bring out the best in his models, finding the positions, expressions and the lighting needed to enhance their looks Victoria emerged from these sessions feeling wrung out, but happy. With his beautiful Italian accent and his patience, Tony incited them, like an animal tamer, to perform for the camera. He prowled about like a feline, trying to capture the smallest detail. His words were like caresses. Today's session took place on a beach close to a cliff, in a heavenly spot. She was supposed to roll about lasciviously by the water's edge, her body and face dripping, then crawl along the cliff like a wild beast.

"That's perfect, like that. Don't move, look at me," she heard him say.

It lasted for hours. A whole team was there: the makeup artist, the hairdresser. Orders were given, gently but firmly. Tony was passionate, but communicated a sense of ease. In a word, he made them beautiful. He confessed that he preferred working with Victoria, because she was sensitive, intuitive, receptive, superbly "built", and knew how to make her body and everything she wore vibrate. Like a creeping vine, she entwined herself around the camera's focus. She had grace, sensuality, and a piercing look that captured the light.

Marco, the handsome "corsair", continued to court her during the rare breaks from work, but she remained insensitive to his advances. She knew this kind of seducer, with their games and their selfishness. They inflamed women's hearts, and then disappeared. They were pyromaniacs who could cause considerable damage. Most of them ended up marrying women without any connection to their past. These women mothered them, put up with their whims, pampered them like gods. Usually, this worked out well. The women produced handsome children and succeeded where others had failed. They directed and commanded, while the former machos, as time passed, became their lapdogs! But Victoria was different: romantic, passionate, and exclusive, she needed to trust and admire the man that she loved. Was that so difficult to find?

Alexandre

On her return to Paris, Victoria had only one idea in her head: Pierre. When she arrived at her apartment, she pushed the button on her answering machine, which contained an impressive number of messages. All of them from Pierre! Had he been deliberately trying to saturate the machine? He seemed to be going crazy. He'd received her letter and wanted to see her, discuss things. Explanations? What for? She could already picture the scene. She knew herself: she could be virulent and saw herself saying pitiless things dripping with acid. No, it would be grotesque. She might as well end things with dignity. In the last messages, his tone became more aggressive, both clumsy and threatening. He must have been drinking. She decided that she would have to change her telephone numbers, both the one at home and her cell phone's. She had to make a clean break. She'd loved him passionately, but now things were different. The image of the pretty girl he'd been with haunted her thoughts and tortured her pride. She called her brother, wanting to hear his voice. He was in London for business, but was planning to return to Paris for the weekend.

"Are you coming on your own?" she asked timidly.

Alexandre was surprised at the tone of her voice. He knew his sister and sensed something was wrong.

"Yes. Keep Friday evening reserved for me. And ask Henriette to prepare the apartment for my arrival. She told me the workmen have finished the repairs. None too soon!"

She announced that she was going to change her telephone numbers. He didn't ask any questions. He was tender and affectionate, as always. When she hung up, she felt a lump in her throat. She had forgotten all about... But never mind! The main thing was that he should feel good about himself and come to terms with his homosexuality.

As agreed, Alexandre came by to pick her up at 9:30 p.m. Unable to find a place to park, he called her with his cell phone to tell her he was waiting for her down below. She arrived, looking radiant, wearing her most beautiful smile. She was so happy to see him.

"What a vision! You dazzle me every time I see you," he said, giving her a kiss.

She was proud of her brother. Always so elegant, refined, and thoughtful. His subtle scent, mixed with the odor of the leather seats in the car, made a fragrance she found pleasant to breathe. He always had funny anecdotes to tell her. Victoria relaxed. He adored her bursts of laughter.

The Coste restaurant, as usual, was full. Their table wasn't ready yet. The hostess proposed that they have a drink in the bar. An S-shaped armchair welcomed them into its arms... The position wasn't very comfortable, but it was romantic... Alex ordered two glasses of champagne. They both smiled at the idea of finding themselves together that evening like two lovers. They spoke with their eyes meeting eyes. His deep handsome gaze seemed to be searching out the hidden corners of her heart. She liked to listen to the vibrations of his voice, to drink in the light of his eyes, and admire the gracefulness of his gestures. The fusion she achieved with her brother had always approached perfection, on the emotional, intellectual, and spiritual planes. There was a cosmic phenomenon between them, where they shared the same wavelength. They adapted, matched, and were receptive to one another. They were in complete harmony. Their neighbors no doubt thought they were in fact lovers and looked upon them with envy. They made such a handsome couple! They weren't unaware of the reactions they provoked. Accomplices, they were enjoying the game. During the meal, Victoria confided in him. At certain points while she was talking, he took her hand and brought it to his lips. She told him of Pierre's betrayal. Alex listened attentively, trying to minimize Pierre's fault. But his sister was adamant. Calm and relaxed, she told him that Pierre was no longer the love of her life. She depicted for him the Prince Charming of her dreams and told her brother that her thirst for love could not be satisfied by a mere drop of water. An arrow aimed at Pierre... That made Alex smile. *How beautiful she is when she's melancholy*, he could not prevent himself from thinking. She was everything he loved: his feminine ideal. If he found a girl who met the same criteria as Victoria, he would marry her without hesitation! She noticed his inner turmoil.

"What are you thinking about, Alex?"

"About you. You're very beautiful, Victoria, a real woman now. You are going to make lots of men suffer!"

"I think the same about you," she replied with a half-smile. "The woman who marries you will be very lucky."

Alex once again took his sister's hand and bestowed upon it a furtive kiss, all the while watching her velvet eyes. A disturbing shiver ran through Victoria's body.

"I'm very jealous of Pierre and the other men who court you. To some extent, you belong to me. We're of the same blood, made from the same flesh. I know your dreams, your anxieties, and your desires."

"Don't be so sure, Alex, you knew all that when we were children. But you don't share my secrets now... And I don't share yours," she said in a serious tone.

Alex did in fact notice she was different tonight. That nostalgic mood causing her eyes to shine with an inner fire made her extremely attractive... He wanted to take her into his arms and hold her tightly. When they got up from the table to go to the cloakroom, a ravishing creature approached Alex. From the look she gave him, Victoria guessed that something had gone on between them. She moved away discreetly, going to the patio to admire the romantic terrace. She loved this place. When Alex found her, her eyes were lost in thought. He took her by the shoulders and led her to the exit. The bellboy arrived with the car. It was about 1 a.m. when he dropped her off in front of her building. Gallantly, he got out of the car to open the door for her and accompanied her to the porch. Victoria punched in the access code, thanked her brother for dinner, and offered her cheek to say goodnight. At that instant, he drew her to him, and kissed her on the lips. Victoria was startled. One of her earrings fell to the ground. She stooped down to pick it up – allowing her to mask her astonishment.

"*Ciao!* See you tomorrow," she said without looking at him.

She hastily entered the lobby of her building, her heart pounding hard. She wiped her lips automatically. In the elevator, she looked at herself in the mirror: she was

livid and her hands trembled. God, his lips were sweet...
She had trouble getting the key into the lock. Her head
was in a muddle. After having put her coat away in the
closet, she went up to her bedroom and headed straight
for the bathroom. The telephone rang. It was her brother
calling her from his cell phone.

"Victoria, I had a marvelous night. I don't know what
came over me, you made me lose my head."

He told her wonderful things that soothed her like a
sweet melody. She lay down on her bed to be able to
listen to him better. She felt unfamiliar sensations,
emanations, an inexpressible radiance. He asked her
which side of the bed she slept on. Victoria's eyes
widened in astonishment. He really had lost his head!
And yet, he'd only drunk at most two or three glasses of
wine.

They went on talking this way until 4 a.m.! Tears rolled
down her cheeks, she was overwhelmed. A strange
feeling flowed within her and made her head spin. Life
was unfair: why did it have to be her very own brother
who talked this way?! She had trouble getting to sleep
afterwards and her pillow ended up being badly bruised.
She had a dream which moved her profoundly. Love
was waging an erotic battle within her. She was making
love to Pierre, whose face became that of her brother.
The result was magical. The caresses and the comings-
and-goings of his muscular body, his words of love, his
sweet, perfumed skin, his precise gestures of an
accomplished lover drew soft moans of happiness from
her.

She awoke in a stupor, frightened by this vision of
amorous delights. The scene from her dream, in all its
details, still danced before her opened eyes. She needed

time to free her senses from a half-numbness. Her body was covered in sweat, shaking with desire. Everything went dark inside her. Had her subconscious provoked this incestuous dream? "Dreams and delusions emanate the same source: the repressed; the dream is the best path to knowledge of the unconscious psyche". She thought the quotation was from Freud.

The following morning, Alex woke her at around ten o'clock. She tried to maintain a natural, detached voice. Above all, she needed to prevent him from discovering how badly he'd upset her. He announced that he was going to meet some friends in Deauville.

"Do you want to come with me?"

Alex's tone was not very inviting and he seemed bothered by something. He must have planned this weekend beforehand. Victoria set him at ease:

"I'm sorry. I would be thrilled to go, but unfortunately I promised some friends that I'd dine with them. Another time, perhaps."

Of course, that was false. She hung up with a pang in her heart. She was sure he was going off with the handsome guy she'd seen in her apartment. She had clairvoyant powers of intuition that detected the secret realities hiding behind appearances and she'd never been proved wrong before. It was a formidable talent that she'd possessed from birth. She decided to leave for Florence to spend a long weekend with friends. Perhaps she would be able to smooth over the sense of uneasiness that clung to her since the previous evening and her dream.

But in Florence things were worse. The image of Alex pursued her at every street corner. His voice resounded in her head. Michelangelo's *David* seemed to resemble him in a troubling fashion. For Victoria, it was a true ordeal. She saw Alex everywhere. That wasn't so surprising, given their Italian origins... The charm of Italian males is irresistible, they have a look that makes women feel more beautiful. She tried to desperately to forget her brother, but his image continued to pursue her madly. Why had she left without telling him?

Victoria wanted to flee from this feeling that grew inside her, enveloping her skin and waking an unhealthy desire within her body. This sensation froze her to the very core. How could such a monstrous thing be happening? It was horrible! Her heart beat wildly and waves of anxiety, guilt, and loathing submerged her. She felt pierced to the depths of her soul. Hardy brambles, with sharp thorns and evil-smelling flowers, had thrust their roots into the arteries of her heart. Her only desire now was to meet someone who pleased her and made her forget all about these fantasies.

Tatiana

Back in Paris once again, her work absorbed her entirely. She was caught up in a flurry of fashion shows, which left her no possibility to feel sorry for herself. It was the best cure for her ailments. Her agenda was fully booked. The agency that employed her appreciated her professional skills and her serious approach. It was true that she was much sought after by the major designers. They said she had charisma and that she made their designs vibrant... And yet a wave of girls from Eastern Europe, as beautiful as suns but cold as glaciers, had invaded the fashion market. They all presented the same look: tall, with angelic faces, fair eyes, and long, golden hair... Immensely long legs, narrow pelvises, and ravishing small buttocks. They made men melt! Victoria worked a lot with a certain Tatiana, who confided in her one day when she was feeling blue, between shots of vodka...

Born in the middle of Russia, oppressed by poverty, Tatiana was twenty years old. She had worked in the fields to help her parents survive. From a man who traveled through the villages seeking pretty country girls to make into stars, in order to exploit them, she learned that there was a fashion models' school in Moscow. He was seductive and a sweet talker. After having flattered her sense of pride in her beauty, he told her that she had all the requisites to become a model and leave behind her ghetto. He claimed to believe in her potential. He even proposed to advance her the money for the journey to Moscow, and would pay for the first months of her classes.

"You'll return the money to me when you start to work," he said.

When opportunity knocks, you have to seize it. Not only was Tatiana beautiful, but above all she was intelligent. She knew that this miserable rural life was not for her. But if she wanted to escape and avoid becoming stuck in poverty like the rest of her family, she would have to leave as quickly as possible, before her beauty deserted her, fading away due to hard labor. She saw no other way out. The adventure promised by Dmitri and his fine words frightened her, but also tempted her. So she followed him to Moscow. He introduced her to Liouba, who directed a famous agency. Tatiana was about to receive a detailed lesson from the school of life. Madame Liouba was in fact very kind to her girls. She taught them how to deport themselves, how to dress, how to manage their hair, and how to use makeup. She was a great teacher. She also taught them, to Tatiana's astonishment, the art of love. To know how to seduce men...

"Your objective," she told them, "once you are in Europe, is to go to the essence of things! That is, you should find a rich man who will take care of you. You have two means of achieving this: your intelligence and your beauty. Men of great importance do not like stupid women. The most clever among you, if you know how to handle matters with patience, charm, and finesse, will obtain marriage. You can't afford to offer yourselves a romance that will take you back to square one. To reign, you need to keep a cool head, never forget that. After having trained with me, you will be ready for the great adventure. You have to create your own luck and give your destiny an extra push."

Indeed, Tatiana told Victoria, the girls left Madama Liouba's with all the tools needed to turn a man's head. Her earnest students learned that the secrets of love were their best chance to survive and succeed in life. Tatiana even confided that to make a man fall in love, one must know how to fake emotion. Tatiana was looked after by an extremely wealthy American, married with three children, whom she'd met at a private party in Paris. This man lived in New York, but came over regularly for business. He was crazy about her.

"I make believe that this is true love, but I don't feel anything for him. He's bought my body, but he doesn't own my heart. He is very generous. Thanks to him, I can rent a nice studio; every month he sends me a handsome amount straight to my bank account. This permits me to help my family, to send them money, because they live in misery. They don't have enough to eat, or to dress well, or to heat their house. This injustice gives me all the courage I need to stop me from going back. 'The more a man is generous with you, the more he respects you. Men despise girls who are for free,' Madame Liouba said."

"It's she who thinks that way," Victoria replied. "I bet today she's old and lonely, your Madame Liouba. There are, thank God, men who think differently. It's much healthier to make love for the pleasure of loving! I feel sorry for you, you talk like a kept girl. It's a sordid way to pass the dawn of your youth. And love with a capital "L", what happens to that? It's the most beautiful thing in the world, to love and to be loved."

"First of all, I need to find a place in the sun and pay off my creditors."

"You have debts?" asked Victoria, intrigued.

"We're protected. They sent us here. We have duties towards them. It costs a lot. They make great demands on us. If we don't go along with them, we risk our lives. It's thanks to them that I'm here. They gave me a chance to succeed. But they follow us closely, they watch us. We are their prisoners. We have no choice, we're caught in a trap."

"Have you ever experienced true love?"

"No, never. I don't even know what it's like to love. I only had a little crush when I was fifteen. He left for the army and I never saw him again. Next, I met Dmitri, the one who introduced me to Liouba. I found out that his job was to recruit girls like me. He seduces them, then..."

A shadow of sadness darkened Tatiana's angelic face.

"My body does not yet know the thrill of love, the most mysterious tumults of the flesh, nor any real carnal passion... I don't even expect any of that can exist one day for me. You can't put faith in the unknown, or calculate the unpredictable. One thing is certain: the day that I find happiness, I will no longer control my destiny. It will be him who holds the reins!"

"Why are you confiding in me like this?" Victoria asked.

"I need to tell someone. I feel so alone in Paris. You are a girl who can be trusted. I've had time, during our work, to observe you and appreciate you. You're different from the others. I see that you are discreet, secretive, intelligent, and generous. You move in a world of light, with a natural grace and ease I do not have. You even intimidate me, a little bit. In short, I would like to be like you."

She added, "I met a boy, a month ago. He came up to me in the street. I found him to be very nice and agreed to have a drink with him. And since then, I've moved into his apartment. He's thirty-two and directs a big ad agency. He's a handsome boy, intelligent, even brilliant. He's been showering me with gifts."

"Are you in love with him?"

"Not at all! But he's kind, generous, and very endearing. He's crazy about me. He's even ready to marry me!"

"After only a month?"

"Yes. I told him that if he loves me like he claims, he should marry me. I put pressure on him because I need to regularize my papers. I added that my American friend was very rich – this is true - , and that he is ready to do anything for me, even divorce his wife so he can marry me."

"What was his reaction?"

"He said he loved me, that he couldn't live without me. He even presented me to his parents. Unfortunately, his mother didn't like me, she refused our marriage, and she no longer wants to receive me in her home. That's all right, I'll achieve my goal, because Patrick is young and he's not unattractive. I am lucky to have met him; I feel that I am capable of making him happy and perhaps even love him someday. I often have changes of mood, anxieties, and crying fits for no reason. It's homesickness, I feel uprooted, and I miss my parents; I also feel guilty about this boy, because I'm not honest with him and he does not deserve this. In short, I'm unhappy. But I want to get ahead, become a student, so that later I can succeed on my own without needing anyone."

She stopped for a moment, then continued:

"In Moscow, I used to meet the wives of important people during dinner parties or at shows. I admired their social success, many of them were of modest social origins like myself... They had made good marriages, had beautiful children, and were in love with their husbands. A dream come true! But they had gone through too many upheavals to have any sense of pride or humility left. They knew that the wheel turns and that they could once again find themselves in my place."

"Go to the essence of things", Madame Liouba had told them. Tatiana was a good student. She wanted to succeed by all possible means, like her older compatriots. Thanks to their well-organized racket, they always managed to place their hooks in men's hearts, and between their legs... . Some of them had even conquered the American market! The richest and the most powerful men behaved like lapdogs around. They had two, three, or four men chasing after them. They made these men suffer, often ruined them, and even used blackmail sometimes... They'd been to a good school! They were a power to be reckoned with, all the while pretending to be frightened rabbits. Tatiana told her about a certain Natasha she knew who lived in New York, beautiful enough to tempt the gods and well-known in fashion circles, who ate caviar by the ladle and drank only the best champagne, who was dressed by the top designers and smothered in jewels. Two famous men were on their knees, calling her ten times a day. She made each of them believe that he was the most marvelous man in the world. And it worked!

According to Tatiana, their network was worldwide. Upon arriving in a country, they had to make themselves known in order to gain access to most exclusive and privileged circles. They had a platinum key that opened even the most strongly protected doors: their beauty. They used it to their maximum advantage. To them, it was a way of taking revenge for their miserable pasts.

Victoria listened to her, dumbfounded. She felt shivers run through her. This angelic face had a veritable computer hidden inside. Her pale green eyes were as cold as a snake's. To be sure, she had suffered, but her heart was cut from stone. That was the reason why Tatiana was not happy in life. She was always complaining about her health. These girls, despite the brainwashing they'd received and which they continued to receive, were fragile. Their moods were cyclical, because they were disoriented. They were always lacking something because they were forbidden from living a true love story: to love and to be loved. This tale chilled Victoria, but she tried as best she could to hide her disappointment from Tatiana. It was really none of her business, she had no right to judge the Russian girl and she even felt pity for her, because she sensed that the other girl was very disturbed.

What Tatiana had omitted from her confession was her attachment to Dmitri. This man, who had supposedly helped her at the start, now controlled both her money and her life! Tatiana told her that when she arrived in France, she lived at a Russian friend's who left her his house because he traveled a lot... Victoria believed this house was the temporary base for some refugees, waiting to be fixed up, with their visas in order..

Melancholy

Several times, Victoria ran into Pierre. He watched for her, followed her, and even ran into her by surprise. He demanded her love, told her that he loved her, said he couldn't live without her, that she should forgive him for that brief fling of no importance. That she was the only one who counted in his life. He even asked her to marry him. But Victoria remained indifferent to his pleading. She did not love him any more, it was futile to pursue their liaison further. She was unhappy for him, she suffered because of this failure. She would have wished with all her might that the love she had felt for him could spring forth again. But when it came to Pierre, love remained not just deaf but frozen like a block of ice.

Love cannot be commanded, it's love that commands, and love alone. It is the master of the universe and does what it will, accord to its mood or its fancy... Sensitive souls beware, lest you be trapped! Love is strong and exceedingly sadistic at times, it can surprise you when you least expect it. When it catches a prey in its net, it keeps its prize; the more it resists, the more love takes pleasure in its torments. And then it's often far too late to retreat. Even the most intelligent, the most clever, and the most powerful people, those who say they are sure of themselves, are vulnerable. So it's been since the dawn of time.

Victoria couldn't help thinking about those fortune-huntresses from Russia, with their angelic faces and ferocious hearts, who looked like butter wouldn't melt in their mouths. The day that love trapped them, they, too, would break into a thousand pieces.

But why was she thinking of that now? Was some danger lying in wait for her? Was the dream she'd had the other night still troubling her? Fortunately, its memory was beginning to fade. Her brother had gone to the United States for a month – that would allow her to put her ideas in order. The telephone rang, wrenching her from her thoughts. She'd left the answering machine switched on: it was Alex! Telepathy at work....

"Vic? Vic, are you there? It's me. No, you aren't there! Too bad! I'm in New York for..."

Victoria hesitated to answer him, but the urge was too strong and she hurriedly picked up the phone.

"I'm here, Alex! I just got home."

"I'm happy to hear you, my little princess. You're my ray of sunshine when I hear your voice. Business is very difficult right now, but I think I just won a big contract. If I finalize it, I'll take you on a beautiful trip."

"A Caribbean cruise? That's my dream!" she said in a cheerful voice.

"Why not? But if that cruise really tempts you, I don't need to wait until the contract is signed. I'll take you whenever you like."

Victoria, surprised by this response, remained speechless.

"Hey, are you still there?" he said ironically.

"I'm here! But I don't like you making fun of me."

"But I'm serious, you know that. I'll do anything to fulfill your desires. You are my eyes, my whole life. You're my favorite birthday present! Don't forget that we were born on the same day... not the same year, fortunately!"

"Why 'fortunately'?"

"I like being your elder brother for many reasons, that I'll keep secret."

"What a macho you are! I recognize you, now!"

"I'm back in Paris next week, reserve me a lunch with you. Thursday, for example, are you free?"

"I'll arrange things."

After conversing several minutes with him, she hung up sadly. 'You're my favorite birthday present. I'll do anything to fulfill your desires.' The words echoed in her head. If only Pierre had used that kind of language. But instead, since their breakup, he hadn't stopped moaning about having lost her, that he loved her, and couldn't live without her...

Victoria's morale was reduced to zero, she couldn't bear anything, everything annoyed her. She felt fed up and tired. It was true that all the fashion shows had left her feeling somewhat drained. She wanted to go away and rest for a few days: it would do her the greatest of good.

It was autumn, Paris shivered under a thin, sticky rain. The people she saw in the street emanated a lugubrious sadness. It was rare to see any elegant-looking individuals: they covered up rather than dressed up! It was also the era of "phonemania". At every street corner, while crossing the road, in their cars, they talked with their cell phones stuck to their ears. Some laughed, others cooed, insulted, or gesticulated. Observing them, one would have said they were madmen who had just gotten out of an asylum. And to think that she did the same thing herself! Such was progress, a new era where easy communications created solitude. You no longer saw people, you phoned them. It wasn't very romantic. It was all just noise in the wind...

In the meantime, Alex left a message from New York confirming his arrival and lunch. Thursday came, it was noon and there still was no word from him. He had specified a time and place to meet. She worried about his silence, but didn't call him back. At 12:15, the phone rang: it was him.

"Vic, I'm sorry to call you so late. Do you still want to have lunch?"

"Of course! I've left lunch open for you," she said crossly.

"All right, I'll come pick you up."

He arrived several minutes later and sat down in the armchair. To Victoria's great surprise, he looked worried.

"Where do you want to have lunch?" he asked, looking at his watch.

Victoria almost choked. It was not usual for him to leave things unplanned.

"I have no idea. If you like we could eat at the Polo Club in Bagatelle park, and enjoy this gentle sunshine which we don't usually get this time of year. Too bad there's no polo match today! I adore that place."

"Me, too. What an excellent idea!"

Victoria avoided putting on a glum face, but her brother's attitude disappointed her. He must not have closed that contract... But being discreet, she asked him no questions. The unique Polo Club, located in a wonderful site full of greenery and flowers close to the very heart of Paris, and with its welcoming, courteous staff, was soothing balm for Victoria's heart. When William, the director of this magical place, came by to say hello, Alex relaxed. Victoria admired her brother. He knew the art of smiling and making other people smile. He was a real charmer. His gaze and his laugh were full of life. But it was troubling that they could no longer behave like brother and sister. Despite themselves, there was an epidermal, physical attraction that they couldn't quite manage to control. It revealed itself in a furtive look or a brush of hands. The situation had almost become intolerable. Alex looked at his watch several times. He said he had an important meeting at 3:30 p.m. She felt disappointed because she would have liked to have taken a walk with him in the countryside. Found a small inn to pass the night. Woken up to the birds singing... She imagined dinner in front of a fireplace... and the decor of the room: old-fashioned, romantic, wall-papered with big flowers...

"It's too bad you have that meeting. I would have liked you to take me for a ride in the country... It's so warm out today," she said dreamily.

He looked at her with a pensive air. He smiled but did not reply. Victoria realized the error that she had just made. He hated it when other people took the initiative. He needed for the desire to come from him. It was the egocentric side of his nature. She tried to make up for it clumsily.

"In any case, even if you had proposed it, I couldn't: I have a meeting with my agent."

He knew his sister well, her reactions; she was fighting with herself. He found her changed, fearful, and mistrustful. She no longer acted naturally with him. She'd become rather secretive. He made a big mistake by playing the seduction game despite himself. He was caught in his own trap and was very attracted by her, to the point of feeling dizzy around her. He desired his sister, a violent desire that woke him in the middle of the night. Any contact with her unleashed impulses within him that he had trouble controlling. He, who was only attracted by other men! Why did life have to play such a monstrous trick upon him? His own sister!

It would be terrifying if Bernard, his friend, ever discovered the truth. He was in any case less and less fooled, constantly asking embarrassing questions or becoming terribly jealous and causing a scene. Alex had tried to break up with him, but Bernard had then attempted suicide. He felt guilty about it: Bernard was a wonderful boy full of good qualities and Alex had no wish to see him suffer. But since he'd discovered the feelings and physical attraction that he had for his sister, something was blocked up inside him. Victoria was his life, his reason for living, his greatest love... How could he get out of this mess? What would be her reaction if she ever discovered his homosexuality? He thought she suspected, but she was too discreet to question him. A trip to Asia, very soon, would allow him to step back from the situation, to disconnect in order to recover his wits. At least, he hoped so.

Angel or demon ?

A month passed. Alex made no attempt to contact her. Victoria went out frequently and she even tried to patch things up with Pierre, in order to forget about her brother. But the dream was broken, it was no longer like before between them. For his part, Pierre was very much in love with her, to the point of losing his reason and plunging into alcohol. He became more and more awkward, aggressive, and even mean. He could not understand why, after having belonged to him, Victoria now resisted him. It made him furious. He called her in the middle of the night, insulting her in his drunkenness. Victoria was terrorized, she didn't need this. She would have liked him to be tender and patient. But she couldn't ask for the impossible from a man who suffered in his love and his pride, to the point of upsetting his mental balance. The fact that he'd started drinking repelled her and diminished him in his eyes as she watched him lose control. She had admired him so much! She tried in a kindly way to reason with him, urging him to give up drinking, telling him he was ruining his health. These words only made him more angry and worsened their relationship. She became impatient for her brother to return from Asia, to be able to confide to him her fears concerning Pierre and ask his advice. But really, it was none of his business and he himself was very discreet about his private life. He no longer told her anything, whereas once they'd traded secrets.

"He'll be arriving any time now, he called me to ask me

to prepare his apartment," his housekeeper, Henriette, confirmed to her.

Victoria felt lonely, misunderstood, and abandoned. Fortunately, her agency was sending her to Venice the following day. This trip would help change her mood, she'd never been to that city before. She was invited to some big parties. Perhaps she'd meet the love of her life there. Who knows? Just as she was getting ready to pack her suitcases, the phone rang. It was Alex.

"Victoria, can I come by to have a drink at your place?"

"I'm sorry, Alex, I can't invite you over. I'm packing because I have to leave very early tomorrow morning. You remember? I told you about this trip to Venice when we had lunch at the Polo Club, you even noted down the date!"

Alex insisted. He wouldn't stay for long, just time to give her a kiss. Faced with his determination, Victoria didn't dare to refuse, although she was somewhat annoyed. She had refused to dine with friends so that she could prepare her baggage in peace. She still hadn't picked out the clothes she would be taking with her. Alexandre arrived within five minutes of his phone call. When Victoria opened the door for him, he hugged her very tightly in his arms.

"I was afraid that you'd gone out to dinner with friends and that I wouldn't get to see you before you leave."

Victoria looked at him in surprise, even astonishment. Her brother was sincere, he was deeply moved. Victoria started to understand. Alex had been trying to flee from her – that explained his silence. But the idea that she was leaving for Venice and his knowledge of his sister's weakness for Italian charm had filled him with panic. His jealousy, an irrefutable proof of love, had woken him to the cold, hard truth. A battle had started between them against the taboo. Which of them would break it? It was forbidden to love those of the same flesh and blood. For Victoria, the struggle against herself was beyond her powers. That day more than ever, only Pierre could have saved her, but it was too late. The waiting list of her suitors was long, but none of them aroused any feelings in her. Alex had taken the special place in her secret garden. She could attempt to reason with herself, but the love she felt for her brother was so strong, so violent, and so devastating that it flourished in all the pores of her body. In the morning, she felt anxious, her sobs choked her as soon as she woke. She implored Heaven to sweep away the black clouds that stained her soul. In her brother's embrace, she succumbed to the desire that invaded her. She no longer heard his words, only the beating of his heart. Nevertheless, she reacted, freeing herself from his embrace.

"What would you like to drink? Champagne, vodka?"

"And you?"

"I'd like vodka."

"Good idea. Me, too."

Was she going crazy? Vodka had an aphrodisiac effect on her.

It took all these years for me to realize that I was in love with my own brother! Until that famous dinner at Coste's, nothing foretold of this disaster. We had a wonderful, untroubled, healthy relationship. Never, but never, would I have imagined such an inconceivable situation. Alex joined her in the kitchen as she opened the door of the freezer to take out the bottle of vodka. He seized her by the waist and kissed her affectionately on the neck...

"You're more and more beautiful, my darling little sister."

"My brother is not too bad, either!"

Sitting together on the sofa, they conversed calmly, talking about their projects. They each had a glass of vodka, then another. Not being used to drink, her mind soon became fogged. Suddenly, in the middle of the conversation, her brother interrupted her:

"Come sit closer to me."

In one other's arms they no longer said a word, lost in their thoughts. Alex gently caressed her arm, then, without realizing it, he gripped it nervously. He was hurting her, but Victoria did not dare move. She knew he was fighting with himself. Indeed, Alex had the impression that he was going crazy – the desire for his sister was very strong, her perfume was intoxicating him, her skin was so sweet, and he felt that beautiful body trembling against his own. The vodka was making his head spin. He pulled himself together and looked at his watch.

"Already nine o'clock? My God, they're expecting me for dinner."

Disappointment could be read on Victoria's face.

"Stay here, don't go..."

"You want me to stay?"

"Yes, please."

"Would you be an angel or a demon?'

"Both of them at once," she said with a smile.

Alexandre got up.

"I'll be back, just give me a moment to call my friends. I left my address book in the car."

During his absence, Victoria took the opportunity to empty the ashtray. She leafed through a magazine. The time passed, almost half an hour, and Alex still hadn't returned. She looked out the window, but couldn't see his car. She called his cell phone, but it was switched off. She guessed that he had a rendezvous with a lover, which he couldn't break. The climate that reigned between them had been too ardent and he'd preferred to flee. She tidied the room, fluffed up the cushions on the sofa, put away the glasses, closed the shutters in the living room, turned off all the lights, and was about to go up to her bedroom when she heard the bell. It was him! He'd come back. Her heart beating fast, she opened the door. He looked at her in surprise, everything was bathed in darkness. Confused, Victoria confessed to him:

"I thought you'd changed your mind..."

"I'm not a boor! Who do you take me for?"

He had his briefcase with him...

"You've already cleaned up? I bet you even vacuumed!"

She burst out laughing.

"You crazy man! You've been gone for over half an hour."

"As long as that? I had a hard time getting free: a friend wanted to see me at all costs, he's in the middle of a depression."

Victoria pretended not to hear him.

"Smoked salmon with *blinis*, a fruit salad, and pistachio ice cream that you like so much. Is that all right? I'm leaving tomorrow, I hadn't planned on dining here this evening."

"That suits me perfectly."

Victoria went into the kitchen.

"Wait, I'll help you."

"No, sit yourself down in the living room, watch some

television. I'll take care of everything."

As she set the table in the dining room, Victoria observed Alex. A glass of vodka in one hand, a cigarette in the other, he was watching the news on TV. She sensed that he was happy and relaxed. She adored his presence, he lightened the whole atmosphere of a house. After a few minutes, he got up to help her, as if he could not bear to see her busy on her own.

"We'll put everything on the table, that way we won't have to keep getting up every minute."

"As you wish. But I'll still have to get up to fetch the ice cream..." she said, teasingly. "Do you want to dine with champagne?"

"Personally, I prefer to continue with vodka. And you?"

"Me, too."

With him, everything was simple.

"What are you thinking about, little sister? You're looking thoughtful."

"Stop calling me 'little sister'!

At the tone of her voice, Alex looked at her, surprised.

"Do you prefer me to call you 'princess', like when we were children?"

"Excuse me. Call me what you like. We're fine here, don't you think?"

"With you, I'm always fine," he said pensively.

This dinner by candlelight went pleasantly, as if they were in fact two lovers. They exchanged their ideas and their projects. At the end of the meal, he helped her clear the table and put away the dishes. After they cleaned up the kitchen, he took her by the waist and led her back to the living room. The contact of his hands through her dress troubled her deeply. She tried to pull herself together by thinking that it was her own brother holding her this way. A strange sensation flowed within her. She'd drunk too much vodka, that was obvious. Alex's hand climbed up her back, brushing her gently, and caressed her hair.

"You're very beautiful, very attractive," he murmured. "You are the blue orchid that lights up my dreams... If you weren't my little sister..."

They were standing in the living room, lit only by the candelabra that shed a golden light. She looked at him with her bright eyes, smiling at him tenderly. This quiet atmosphere, Victoria's beauty, that splendid body that he saw trembling before him made him lose his head. He drew her into his arms and their lips joined, hot, burning... She heard him murmur:

"That's good..."

They were no longer brother and sister at that moment. They were only a man and a woman, possessed by the demon of love.

"Do you want this?" murmured her brother.

"Yes..." Veronica responded in an imperceptible breath.

He took her by the hand and guided her to the bedroom. Everything spun round in Veronica's head, like a beautiful merry-go-round. The romantic decor of the room – its soft lighting, its canopied bed, that feminine touch which gave off a perfume – was a setting made to incite love... Incapable of resisting, stretched out against him, she found herself in the middle of a fog. She closed her eyes, as if she never wanted to wake up. She felt his firm and muscular skin against her body. She dove into the intoxication of love... Alex covered her with kisses as if she were a long desired morsel... Everything spun round her, it was marvelous, violent, and magical. The coming-and-going of his body, his lips, and his caresses.

He wanted to give her all possible pleasures, she was so unreal when she made love! He drank the elixir of her enjoyment, which left a taste of honey in his mouth. The room was plunged into half-darkness, only the full moon reflected in the mirrors lit their lovemaking. The radio softly played one of Victoria's favorite songs: '*Je vais t'aimer comme on t'a jamais aimée*'. The voice of Michel Sardou echoed in the room, fueling the madness that had seized the two bewitched lovers.

Afterwards, they remained tightly embraced, not daring to move for fear of ending the moment. Panting, his eyes closed, Alex caressed Victoria's languid body, rippling with shivers. As he caressed her, he dozed off. *God, he's handsome!*, Victoria remarked to herself. Her whole life she would never forget this memorable night, which she had already immortalized in her secret garden. In the deepest part of herself, she knew that no other man would ever give her as much passion and voluptuousness as what she had just experienced. Their bodies had achieved osmosis, a chemical fusion, beyond anything she'd ever imagined. She caressed Alex's hair, who slowly opened his eyelids. He drew her towards her, and gave her a long kiss on the shoulder. Victoria would have liked him to stay and sleep with her, but she had to get up at dawn, prepare her baggage. Henriette would be coming early tomorrow. She would faint with astonishment if she saw them in bed together. She looked at the time: four o'clock in the morning! She kissed his face, his neck, his torso, lingering at his lips.

"You have to go," she said regretfully.

Without a word, he got dressed. She accompanied him to the door. She did not dare look him in the eyes, her face was red with shame. He drew her towards him and kissed her a long while, before moving off to the elevator. Victoria's heart beat very strongly. God, what had they done? Heaven would punish them for this. This night, she had encountered the Devil, who had offered her a royal banquet, a crystal love on a bed of stars. The candles slowly burnt down in the candelabra. The room looked liked a cathedral of light... After packing her suitcases, she set her alarm: she had only two hours to rest.

The sound of the alarm brought her out of a deep sleep. She woke up slowly, fingers clenching on the sheets. Warmth flooded her face, she felt an unpleasant pain in her stomach, and she was petrified. Had she only dreamed? But the wrinkled sheets still retained the perfume and the memory of their mad night. A feeling of terror and guilt invaded her. Another woman had just been born. Whose fault was it? Hers ? His? Both of them? He should not have seduced her. He knew her secret desires and weaknesses. He'd undressed her soul, she felt soiled down to the very core of herself. She ran a bath and quickly prepared her breakfast. But she couldn't swallow anything, her throat was knotted up. Tears rolled down her face. The telephone rang. It was Alex. His voice sounded worried, but he spoke as if nothing had happened. He asked for her number in Venice so he could call her.

"My love, last night was like a marvelous symphony."

"I feel as though I dreamed it," she replied.

"Are you having regrets?"

"Yes, no... I don't know. Everything's mixed up in my head. The only thing I know is that I regret that you're my brother."

"Me, too. Don't ask yourself too many questions, it's our secret. I kiss you, my princess. I'll call you soon."

He was troubled. Everyday, he called Venice at 9 a.m., the only time when he could reach her. She tried to forget him. But Alex had marked her with a red-hot brand. She could reason with herself, judge herself, criticize herself, get mad at him. But there was no help for her! Every time she heard his voice, something stirred deep inside her and tears of fury welled up in her eyes. Why wasn't there a medication against love's hurt? It was a sickness. One would swallow a pill and the next day all would be forgotten, there would be no more suffering. Medicine had made so much progress in our times, performed so many miracles. But no researcher had thought of curing love! It would relieve millions of human beings from this terrifying evil that ate away at heart and health, and could lead to murder, suicide, alcoholism, and madness. There would be less sick people to take care of. Think how much would be saved by an entire country! The passion for love leads inevitably to torment. She would have to forget about all this, and quickly. But what a lover he was! She understood now why women suffered because of him! She was on a thorny path that could only wound her profoundly. Her position was disastrous. This incestuous relationship resembled a plant that grew on brackish, waterlogged land, that would rot away before even reaching maturity! She was aware of that. But the poison had infiltrated into her skin, like a drug that one cannot do without. At night, the Devil came to wake her from her dreams, disturbing her sleep. He had become incarnated within her. The hardest thing was being unable to confide with anyone about the gravity and horror of her situation. She was passionately in love. She thought, lived, and breathed only for him, and by him

Her partners at work noticed that she had changed. She was sad, melancholy, and pensive – qualities that were not part of her usual temperament. She had the impression that everyone had guessed her secret. When Tatiana, more curious than the others, tried to pry confidences out of her, she invented an affair with a well-known married man. Fiona, one of her best friends, suspected that an event had traumatized Victoria, but found it impossible to pierce the mystery. She had become taciturn and savage, refusing to go out to parties, and locking herself away in total silence. Usually so exuberant and gay, embodying the joy of life itself, she had now become the shadow of her own self. She only existed and activated herself for her work, throwing herself into it like an actress in a theater play. In her job, she was on stage, in the role of a character. It was that side of things that saved her. But Fiona worried, fearing that her friend was having a nervous breakdown.

"Victoria, snap out of it! You're going to make yourself ill. With all the men courting you, who suffer because of you, you have to find the one man who's unavailable and who makes you unhappy. Come down out of your dreams and stop eating your heart out. I don't know who this man is, but I hate him for the harm he's doing you."

"It's not his fault, he doesn't even know that I love him so much. Is it so obvious to everyone that I'm unhappy?"

"One only has to look at you! You don't exactly have joy written across your face! He doesn't make you happy and you're suffering because of him! Have you become a masochist? Have you lost your mind? Forget him, he doesn't deserve you. You're too good for him."

If only she knew... Victoria suffered her martyrdom, not knowing how to control her emotions. It was like navigating in stormy seas, tossed about by contrary winds. She implored Heaven with all her strength to help her find the reason for this cursed passion. When she got back to Paris, Alex pretended to be too busy to see her right away. She let silence settle between them. But she knew her brother, he wouldn't resist for long. And in fact, eight days later she received a phone call, at the moment she least expected it. He invited her to lunch the following day. She accepted. When she arrived at the restaurant, he got up to greet her. Victoria was superb and glowing. And yet she seemed indifferent. Alex looked surprised and somewhat put out. He felt his sister was slipping away from him. He noticed that men were looking at her with interest. She was aware of that fact, too, and played up to it with seductive charm. She felt strong enough to confront the Devil himself. Her eyes sparkled with mischief. *She's like a ray of sunshine, she dazzles me*, he couldn't help thinking.

During lunch, Victoria turned talkative and he couldn't get a word in edgewise. But she amused him, he was never bored with her, and she always had stories to tell. It was a change from all those dreadful women who never stopped complaining about the slightest thing. With her, he forgot about everything, even the time. He looked at his watch: 3:15 p.m. God, already!

"Do you have a meeting?" she said suddenly, looking surprised.

"Yes, at three o'clock! I'm late. Will you excuse me?"

On his cell phone, he called up his secretary to ask if his

visitor had arrived. Indeed, he was already there, she confirmed. Victoria was disappointed: she would have liked to stay a while longer. The chauffeur dropped her brother off at his office, before accompanying Victoria home.

"I'll call you," he said, kissing her.

She watched him move off with sadness. He had not asked if they could have dinner together or if he could come see her that evening. Before, he had been freer, more available to her, he told her everything. Now their relationship had changed. Throughout lunch, she'd bitten her tongue to prevent herself from saying disagreeable things to him. When the heart is inflamed, sparks spray from the mouth. Above all, he must not discover how much she suffered.

When she arrived at her apartment, she found a message waiting for her. Alex asked her if she was free for dinner. She accepted and confirmed on her brother's answering service.

She didn't have any ideas about how she should dress: it all depended on the restaurant he picked. She opted for a ravishing little black dress. She knew her brother, he liked to go with her to fashionable places, especially in the evening. She took care in dressing, so that he would be proud of her.

Satan leads the dance

It was a little after 8 p.m. Alex still hadn't called back, as he usually did. He'd adopted a new attitude towards her that she did not care for at all. He liked to keep people waiting! Then he'd show up when he was not expected. He wanted to surprise people and to control his own desires. The only reproach she could make against him was his egocentricity. Before, he never would have permitted himself to act this way with her. One might say he liked to play this sadistic game in order to discover how his victims would react! She had cancelled a dinner for him. Anger rose within her and she called back her friend to say that she might be free after all. It was easy to understand, from Victoria's tone of voice, that it had been a lovers' rendezvous...

"If he doesn't show, come and join us. I'll give you the address and telephone number. Do you have something to note this down?" Fiona asked.

"Yes, tell me..."

She noted the restaurant's details. Her decision was made, she was going to teach Alex a lesson. Who did he think he was? If he thought he thought he could give her the run-around like other women, he was mistaken. She finished getting ready and was about to call a taxi. The telephone rang, it was him!

"Oh, it's you?" she said, surprised.

"What do you mean, oh it's me?"

"I was about to go meet my friends."

"But we agreed to have dinner together!"

"Have you seen the time? I thought you changed your

mind."

"It's really an obsession with you, isn't? When I promise you something, I keep my word!" he said, offended. "Where do you want to have dinner?"

"What! You didn't reserve a table at a restaurant? At this hour, everywhere will be full!"

"I had an external meeting, I just got finished. Do you really want to go out?"

Victoria controlled her anger. This was the second time he'd tried this. It was once too many.

"Yes, I need to go out and change my frame of mind. Don't worry about me, I'll go join my friends."

"But you don't understand! I've changed my mind, I don't want to go to a restaurant this evening. I'm fed up with restaurants!" Alex said. "I would have liked for the two of us to dine together at home. I want to be alone with you. Do you?"

Victoria felt her anger melt away.

"I'll take care of everything. Do you want a Chinese dinner?"

"Oh, yes!" she said, more cheerfully.

"Perfect. I'll make sure they deliver the order and then I'll come over."

That Alex! Always surprising her. She'd been right to tell him that she wasn't waiting for him any longer. The next time, he'd take care to warn her if he was going to be late. Well, she'd have to get changed again, now! Her tight dress was no longer appropriate, she'd be too provocative. She had no desire to seduce him in the intimacy of her own home. A mysterious rage gripped her. From her wardrobe she chose black satin pants and a little fuchsia top which brought out her good complexion. Alex hated women in pants. A half hour later, the bell rang. Was it him? She picked up the building phone and on the video screen she saw the delivery boy. Already! The boy arrived loaded with packages.

"That's for six people!" she said, stupefied. "Are you sure you haven't mixed up customers?"

"Not at all!" he answered, verifying the invoice.

The delivery boy left and Victoria remained speechless before a veritable feast from the best Chinese caterers in Paris! It must have cost him a lot more than if they had gone to a good restaurant. He'd even taken care to include wine! When he arrived a few minutes later, she remarked in a friendly fashion:

"There's enough to eat for three days!"

"There's everything you like, since I didn't know what you like the most..."

Alex cast an admiring eye at the living room, all lit up and full of flowers. He liked the warm, quiet decor of her very feminine, cozy apartment. This evening, passing in front of her florist's shop, she'd splurged on some bright yellow roses. These fresh roses gave the illusion of a ray of sun breaking through on a gray day. She had lit all the candelabra, put out his favorite cigarettes, as well as the box of cigars from Gérard's in Geneva, who had the best quality brands for real connoisseurs, of whom Alex was one. On the low table, in a silver bucket, a bottle of champagne was stuck deep into a pack of ice cubes... There were two shining crystal goblets and some salted biscuits. She had decorated her table with a pretty lace tablecloth. Before he arrived, she'd given the decor a satisfied inspection, put on some soft music, and lightly vaporized perfume around the room. Everything was in place to receive her Prince.

For a few minutes they sat talking on the sofa while drinking a glass of champagne. Alex said to her, ironically, "I'm surprised to see you in pants..."

"I didn't feel like pleasing you," she said in a joking tone.

He smiled at this sally.

"I'm hungry. What about you?" she said.

He suggested, as on other occasions, that they put everything on the table. The delicious dishes, the champagne, the good wine, all made it difficult for her to keep her head out of the clouds. She had put the lights on out on her circular terrace, still blooming with scarlet geraniums and oleanders. The wisteria provided a tracery of foliage. The thick jasmine climbed along two stone columns, adjoined by an 18th century bronze statue representing a water-carrying goddess. If you couldn't see in the distance the top of the Eiffel Tower rising majestically into the sky, you might have believed that you were in Italy.

"I adore dining in your place, it's nicer than a restaurant, don't you think?"

She smiled out of happiness at being with him that evening. He was so handsome, he was almost unreal.

"Come sit on my knees."

She had to resist him. Nevertheless, she obeyed. She slipped her arms around his neck and put her head on his shoulder, as she had when she was a little girl. She felt so good with him... A strange elixir circulated in their veins. They were joined by a mysterious, indissoluble link. They tried in vain to defend themselves from this cursed love that chained them together despite themselves, unable to find the key that would free them from this irresistible passion. She let out a sigh, wanting to crush this serpent that devoured her entrails. She loved him onto death, onto damnation.

"What's tormenting you?" Alex asked, hugging her more tightly.

"Love for you. Fear of loving you still more, tomorrow..."

He looked at her with eyes aflame, full of fever.

"My love, I love you, our lives are intertwined and knitted together despite ourselves. I can't live without you. I can't control what's happening to us. It's worse than an earthquake. For you, I'm ready for anything, whether it be madness or wisdom. There's a Chinese proverb that says the bottom of the heart lies further than the end of the world. You are the end of the world for me, my beloved."

"But you are my brother!"

"Alas," he sighed.

Was it Heaven or Lucifer that took possession of their souls, their hearts, and their bodies? They had reached a region of love hitherto unknown to them, where they became subject to violent shockwaves. How would they survive this tragedy with no solution? How could they defy hell?

Caressing her long hair, Alex murmured a poem:

If water could extinguish a loving blaze,
Your love that burns me is so strongly painful
That I would put out its fire in the sea of my tears.[1]

"How beautiful! Did you write that?" she asked.

---

[1]   *Si l'eau pouvait éteindre un brasier amoureux,*
       Ton amour qui me brûle est si fort douloureux
       Que j'eusse éteint son feu de la mer de mes larmes.

"Non, it's by Pierre de Marbeuf, a 17th century poet."

"You like poetry?"

"Yes. And you?"

"Me, I nourish myself with it. Poems are the morsels of my soul. I adore, among other things, *Flowers of Evil* by Charles Baudelaire."

The atmosphere became burning. To put out the blaze, Victoria withdrew her arms and started to clear the table.

"Go wait for me in the living room, I won't be long. I bought you the cigars you like."

When she arrived in the living room, she found him smoking his cigar with relish, while enjoying a glass of cognac. He was an epicurian. The power of seduction that he exercised over her made her lose all reason. Their eyes became evasive, then locked in a perilous glance that stirred up the fire that already consumed them. Each of them struggled. Reason fought a cruel battle with desire. The brush of their feverish hands, the epidermal, carnal contact, the fatality of this forbidden love rose above any moral laws. Sitting at the other end of the sofa, she chatted while avoiding his gaze. She was tense and struggled with all her might not to succumb to his bewitching charm. *You idiot, you're going straight to Satan if you give in another time.* The light of the candles illuminated Victoria's face, lending her the beauty of a Madonna. Alex was deeply moved by this. She dazzled him like a sun, she was the apple of his eyes. The temptation to possess her again that night took such a clear hold over his body, setting him completely aflame and burning his senses, that he almost lost his head.

"Come closer to me..."

Victoria hesitated, she looked at him with a distracted

air, but she couldn't resist any longer. Emotion and fright were painted on her face. He drew her to him and held her tightly in his arms, feeling her beautiful body tremble beneath his caresses. They kissed passionately. Their wanting agitated them, embraced them, spilled out of all their senses, like a torrent falling over a cliff, revivifying their guilty love. Victoria's head swayed dangerously as they mounted to the bedroom. Through the half-opened window on which the moonbeams played, the night was shining and clear. The light of the candles produced a reverberation of trembling colors, so beautiful that even the sun after rain could not have painted a more splendid rainbow on their nude bodies. Carnal desire set them aflame. Alex incited her to abandon herself to the frenetic impulses of her sensibility. He felt along with her the sensual perceptions that gripped her flesh. Filled with all the voluptuous pleasures of her touch, the excesses that swelled his desire provoked in him a thousand kinds of madness that fractured any taboos... Victoria's caresses, the satin finish of her skin, her perfume, and her moans all roused in him a current that resembled a sudden irruption of electrical fluid. The fervor did not cease to grow in the spasmodic bodies of the two lovers. In order to augment it still further, they refined the kisses and the caresses through which they mutually fulfilled one another. There was in them an uncontrollable intoxication. They were no longer masters of themselves, perceiving that in the realm of love nothing was prohibited and that everything was sanctified. The bond that entwined them profoundly penetrated their flesh.

The god of Love had shot a poisoned arrow at them. The

passion that Alex procured for her seemed infinite... Their eyes were charged with impetuous messages. Victoria felt herself swept away in a whirlwind of incredible beauty, that toppled her into a forbidden universe. She attained with him a region of ecstasy hitherto unknown to her, where she received ethereal particles of great purity. There existed between them a cosmic force that transported them into an almost magical voluptuousness. Exhausted, drained by this tumultuous night, he had fallen asleep in his body... Victoria did not dare move for fear of waking him and spoiling their embrace... Ashamed, damp with anxious sweat, she quivered at the horror of her act. She had become the slave of a passion that terrorized her and intoxicated her at the same time. Her eyes half-closed, she watched the candles burn down. This sublime love took on the weight of a torture. Outside, a new day rose, while the night slipped away...

Two hearts back to front

Victoria was woken by the sun dazzling her face. It was true that last night she'd forgotten to close the shutters and draw the curtains... She looked at the time: 11:30 a.m. Alex has left... His things were no longer there. No doubt he had not wished to disturb her sleep. She pulled the duvet over head to try and recapture a dream. It was Saturday and she had nothing planned. She went back to sleep.

"Good morning, princess. Wake up, my love."

Was this the continuation of her dream? But his kisses? His caresses? His words of love? That odor of perfumed tea? She opened her eyes: he was really there, sitting near to her, completely dressed. He had deposited upon her bed a royal breakfast tray: croissants, buttered toast, honey, orange juice, and a sumptuous branch of white orchids.

"I couldn't find any orchids with the same color as your eyes..." he said, giving her a kiss on the lips.

Victoria looked at him, feeling moved. What a seducer! And moreover, a poet!

"I hesitated to wake you, you were sleeping like an angel. It's almost noon and I didn't think it was reasonable to let you sleep any longer."

What a dear! He'd gone down to do the shopping! A few moments later, he told her he very much wanted to spend the weekend with her, if she was free, of course. Victoria's blue eyes shone with a thousand sparks. She did not dare believe it, it was too beautiful... Her heart was overflowing with spring.

During those two days of madness that followed, the two lovers would go the very ends of their passion, until they made the very stars blush...

Monday morning, Alex left the apartment at 7:10 a.m., leaving Victoria still sleeping deeply. He did not want to see her waking, it was better this way. He had to go back to his place and change, he had a meeting at 9 a.m. with an important client. His profession as a capital manager engrossed him and took up much of his time, but also put him under a great deal of stress, because the stock market required nerves of steel! He constantly monitored shares prices on his pocket computer, contained in a case the size of a pack of cigarettes! Thus, he could find out the state of the market at any given moment, wherever he found himself.

The love relationship with his sister perturbed him and made him feel guilty. He no longer knew where he was with it, nor what was happening to him. He'd completely lost his head and while he tried to reason with himself, it overpowered him. This love was a luminous beam that projected a burning fire within him. He went from intoxication to an inner feeling that oppressed him and plunged him into extreme affliction. He came to realize a little too late the gravity of his act. Against his will, he had driven himself to despair by taking this dead end path. This blood liaison was destroying him. But the worst thing was that he felt no regret, only remorse. He loved his sister madly, as he'd never loved before.

Lost in his thoughts, he did not see Bernard who was waiting for him in front of his building, nervously smoking a cigarette. He only noticed him as he was getting out of his car. From Bernard's demeanor, he sensed a violent storm was brewing.

"Where were you? I was searching for you all night!"

"I was in the country with friends..." Alex said, opening the carriage entrance.

What bad reflexes! It was not a very original response, he could have found a better one.

"Do you take me for an idiot? Since when did you go to the country wearing a suit? And where's your travel bag?" said Bernard, raising his voice.

Poor Bernard had picked the wrong moment. Alexandre was not in a mood to put up with his comments, and still less his reproaches. He glared at the other man and clenched his jaw, at which point Bernard immediately calmed down.

"I'm in a hurry. If you want, come up with me for a few minutes. We can't have this kind of a discussion in the street, making a spectacle of ourselves;"

Surprised by the tone of his voice, Bernard did as he was told. He was frightened by Alex's crestfallen face. Upon entering the apartment, Bernard searched desperately for a clue that would enlighten him concerning his friend's behavior: dirty glasses, cigarette butts in the ashtray...

"If you want me to be pleasant, make us some coffee while I take a shower."

Bernard was staggered! Alex had reversed the situation with a coldness and off-handed tone that left him speechless. Like a madman, he looked in the trash can to see if there wasn't an empty champagne bottle. He trembled with anger. But everything was clean, tidy, with no trace of a feast...He knew Alexandre well, his liking for independence, his dislike for remonstrance.

Alexandre had been honest with him, fixing the conditions from the very start, which applied as much to the one as to the other. Each of them would live on their own seeing one another only to share agreeable moments. Bernard had accepted, but unfortunately, he had not foreseen that he was going to fall madly in love with Alex, and that was the awful thing. Bernard was a handsome boy, very virile, tall, with brown hair, green eyes, and an athlete's body, muscular and lanky... He also enjoyed enormous success with women and, of course, with men. But Alex had come to occupy an important place in his life. They had met at a party at Castel's, a Parisian club. Bernard headed a film production company.

While preparing coffee, Bernard was in agony, his stomach in knots. He felt a seed of madness climb into his head and murderous thoughts crossed his mind. But when he saw Alex come into the living room, with his drawn features and his closed, livid face, he no longer dared utter any remarks. What grave thing could have happened to put him in such a state? The only reassuring thing was that he wasn't wearing a happy, radiant face, like someone who'd just spent a pleasant weekend!

Much to Alexandre's great relief, Bernard had become more calm, almost relaxed. Now he only had a hangdog look... After drinking their coffee in silence, Alexandre told him he had an important meeting and that he would call him, without confessing that he'd taken a important decision. He had recently been offered a very important post in Singapore, by all accounts an advantageous promotion. He had said he would think about it, that he required a month's reflection. He didn't want to move away from his sister, whom he couldn't imagine on her own, far away from him. Fragile and vulnerable, she had only him to turn to. Of course, that was only a pretext: the truth was he could not live without her. He could no longer have relations with Bernard, or anyone else.

No technique, no remedy, and no science in the world could be of any help against this impossible love, except flight. He knew what his response would be before he spent the weekend with Victoria. It was a farewell tryst. Possessed by a demon, he'd loved her like a madman, in order to take with him a final memory. She was young, beautiful, intelligent, and she would forget him. Shame on him, might he be cursed for having dragged his sister into the flames of hell. To be sure, he should have thought of that sooner. But the spell upon them was so strong that they had succumbed to this forbidden liaison. They could no longer content themselves with an episodic relationship that would shatter them into a thousand pieces and destroy them totally. It was inconceivable. And it was up to Alexandre to take their destiny in hand and save them before it was too late.

That very evening, Victoria received a phone call from Alex. He told her that he had to leave in two or three days on a trip to Asia. This did not surprise Victoria: his brother's work led him to travel throughout the world. To some extent, it was welcome news: everything was so confused in her mind. She was in a complete fog. Her destiny was traversing a violent zone of turbulence that was making her feel nauseous. From the tone of his voice, she wondered if he had not instigated this impromptu journey himself.

He did not ask to see her before his departure – a fact that sharpened her intuition. This incestuous relationship was destroying them, both of them needed to step back from it. To put him at ease, she told him in her most serene voice that she, too, was going abroad for her work. Alex was taken aback by his sister's reaction – and this stabbed at him even more. She had to forget him, she must do so at all costs if she did not want to end her days in an asylum! They'd had great moments together, beautiful moments. If they continued to consummate this mortal sin they would be cursed, Heaven would punish them. Their love had no future. Alex must continue on his path, and she must follow her road.

Alex was unable to tell her the truth about this definitive departure. She would never know what he'd endured. A storm wind blew through his head. He did not want to hurt her. Perhaps with their separation they would come back to their senses and find peace in their souls. They themselves were the artisans of the tragedy that befell them, they themselves ha blindly provoked this terrible tornado in their lives. They themselves, to be sure, but above all, that thing which we call Love.

Bernard

After Alex's departure, Victoria tried to drown her sorrow in a giddy frenzy of work. At times, she also went out clubbing with friends. But that proved worse, she felt terribly alone in the middle of the partying crowd, with that deafening music. No, truly her morale was too low to bear that wild ambience. Her heart was awhirl, traversing a violent storm. She had no one to confide in and his silence only aggravated her distress. What was he doing at that very moment? Was he with someone? He had given her his new cell phone number where she could reach him day or night in case of need. But both of them preferred to respect their pact of silence.

One evening as she was coming home, she ran into the handsome boy she had seen in her apartment, her brother's friend... Apparently, he'd been waiting for her. Upon seeing her, he approached and hailed her discreetly:

"*Bonsoir*. Are you Victoria, Alex's sister?"

She looked at him questioningly.

"My name is Bernard, a friend of your brother's..."

He hesitated, then said, "I won't hide from you the fact that I was waiting for you. I haven't had news from Alex since he left for Asia. I'm worried," he mumbled.

"Come have a drank at my place, we'll be more comfortable than discussing this in the street."

Bernard did not need persuading. Gallantly, he offered to help Victoria with her packages, because her arms were loaded. Bernard wondered if Victoria knew about her brother's love life. As for her, she was asking herself the same question. Both of them were troubled at finding themselves face-to-face. Bernard noticed that almost all of the framed photos in the apartment were of Alex, Victoria, their mother, and their father. And girlfriends. But there was no photo of another man, he was surprised by that.

After having served him a glass of whiskey, Victoria tried to relax the atmosphere by making him talk about his work. Bernard was bothered. Victoria didn't seem to be aware of his relationship with Alex. In order to hear news of Alex, he'd been left with only one solution: his sister! Victoria perceived his tragedy and his wound. He was infinitely sad. She could not even help him, let him know that she was aware of the situation, since she could not permit it with Alex. He was not supposed to know that she'd discovered the truth about them and their liaison. Yet she wanted very much to know more about this relationship. She wasn't jealous, she felt close to him because they shared the same suffering. They loved the same man! Her lips were burning to ask one question. Why did these two men, handsome as gods, prefer men to women? What triggered their choice? They were superb, intelligent, refined, elegant, and courteous. They were princes! They had everything needed to make women's hearts spin! She would have liked to clear up that mystery. Was it the forbidden nature of their love that provoked desire? Perhaps they had greater affinities, a complicity. She thanked nature for having made her a woman! She was at ease with herself, in her head and in her body. She adored man with a capital "M", to the point that if she was a man, perhaps she'd also be a homosexual! So, she should be able to understand Alex, since she thought that way. But no, it was too complex, too ambiguous. Yet, sexually, with him, it had worked divinely, like she was rolling in the clouds... Alex was the opium of her soul. But she wasn't about to let herself off lightly, she judged herself severely and felt guilty, even horrified herself. She had been normal before this cursed love that gnawed her to the bone, preventing her now from ever living happily, having been stained by sin, thinking only of him day and night. Split in two, anesthetized by this passion, Lucifer had set fire to her soul.

As he was chatting, Bernard noticed the sadness in her eyes.

"I'd better go, I don't want to disturb you any longer. Thank you for having received me so kindly," he said as he got up.

"But you haven't disturbed me, quite the contrary. Call me when you like, it would be a pleasure to hear from you."

"Really?"

"Really. I'll tell my brother that we saw one another, I think that would please him... He hasn't called me yet since he left. He must have lots of work, he doesn't usually leave me without news from him."

At those words, Bernard's face brightened. He looked at his watch, it was 8:15 p.m.

"If you have nothing planned this evening, it would be a pleasure to invite you to dinner. It was so good to be with you..."

She looked him right in the eyes, as if to discover his truth. The reflection therein was sincere, he did not drop his gaze, filled with emotion and kindness. She hesitated a moment. What would her brother say?

"I didn't plan on going out this evening. I wanted to rest because I start work early tomorrow morning. But why not? That will give us the opportunity to become better acquainted."

"Do you like Japanese cuisine? I know a very good restaurant not far from here."

"Excellent idea: I adore it!"

What a liar! She would have preferred to eat Italian... When they arrived at the restaurant, the manager came up to them enthusiastically. Apparently, Bernard was a regular customer. He gave them the best table, but Bernard asked for a quieter, more isolated spot. He took them to the basement, to a real lovebirds' nest... Here, it's true that they would be calmer and sheltered from indiscreet eyes...

"We're better off down here to talk, upstairs there's too much noise," he said.

The waiter took their order. Victoria asked Bernard to help her compose her menu. She adored it when a man took initiatives for her, it was a very womanly type of behavior. Men, in general, adored it, too.

"What would you like to drink?" he asked her.

"The same thing as you."

"Bring us tea."

Tea? She'd been expecting him to choose wine... She intervened, slightly flustered, not wanting to drink wine all on her own.

"I would like a beer."

Bernard smiled and ordered the beer. He found her radiant and she gave off an intoxicating perfume. She glowed whenever she spoke. Her eyes, a piercing blue, troubled him strangely. She was very beautiful, attractive, sensual, and exceedingly feminine. He felt comfortable with her, he had the impression that he'd known her a long while, especially since Alex never stopped talking about his sister, boasting about all her merits. He hadn't been exaggerating, on the contrary. *How bizarre life is*, Victoria thought. *Why does it have to be my brother's boyfriend who's here with me?* She found him fascinating, incredibly charming, and full of humor. Too bad... He'd ordered a royal meal. The dishes never ceased coming to their table, each more succulent than the one before. Victoria, who had not been hungry at the beginning, ate greedily. Bernard watched her, touched by her freshness, her naturalness, her ease, and her beautiful smile... When he accompanied back to her home, at the door he asked if he could call her and see her again, to repeat this kind of friendly dinner. Victoria told him that she, too, had spent an excellent evening. In fact, she'd had a very hard time during dinner ignoring certain images that troubled her vision. Alex, Bernard... But his kindness had succeeded in winning her friendship.

The following days, Bernard called her, and he even adopted the habit of asking for her news almost daily. He often invited her to dinner and they became good friends. To Victoria's great astonishment, he spoke no more of Alex. She didn't understand it, and moreover, she did not try. In contrast, she was surprised that he was interested in her. He noticed her sadness, but Victoria invented a story. She was in love with a married man. If only he knew! As for him, he said not a word about his private life, maintaining total silence. It would not be her who would start questioning him! She did not want to know more, at all. But one evening, during the course of a dinner, he confided in her...

"You know, Victoria, when I saw you for the first time, I was utterly confused. I, too, had an unhappy breakup. A direct blow to the heart. But today, I'm healed. That love hurt me too much, and since I'm not a masochist, I've chosen to forget."

"It's not as simple as that for everybody!" Victoria responded. "Love is the king of the Universe. Without it, the Earth would not be a vibrant place, it would not survive. Without water, there would not be life. Love is the water of life! It possesses many facets and only it can decide, you can't fight against its laws. It can stab you at the moment you least expect it. It can mutilate or destroy, if it so desires. When it aims right at your heart, you have a hard time getting back up. Even the most powerful person in the world falls at its feet, vanquished and humiliated. Afterwards, it forgets you, and goes on its way. It's up to us to find the courage and the strength to heal. And perhaps the next love will be the right one..."

Bernard looked at her, surprised by such language. She must have suffered to be saying such things at her age. But there was no age in matters of love and the heart never grows wrinkles... He was still reticent in relation to his homosexuality, with his family and circle of friends. He preferred to hide it and that only made matters worse. Victoria was apparently unaware of it and that suited him. A disturbing thing was happening to him; destiny appeared to playing a funny trick with him. Much to his surprise he discovered that he was thinking night and day about Victoria, to the point of forgetting Alex! What would his reaction be if he ever found out? It was the first time he had felt such strong feelings for a woman and had fantasies about her. To be sure, he'd slept with several girls for the pleasure of it. He must not let Victoria suspect anything about his feelings. He would have to be patient: perhaps one day he would win her heart. For the moment, he did not want to ruin this friendship, he must remain her friend and her confidant.

Victoria in fact suspected none of this. She considered Bernard to be a friend, and she was glad that such a friendship comforted her a little, but it prickled her at the same time! Bernard was so thoughtful with her that she dared not push him away. And then, she was comfortable with him. He calmed her and protected her in his fashion. Whenever she needed him, he was there. Life could be so awkward! He would have been exactly the type of man she needed to weather this difficult passage. To think that if she hadn't surprised the two of them, that one famous evening, she probably would have succumbed to his charisma.

She told herself that she couldn't go on torturing herself. She should consult a doctor, free herself of the enormous weight on her chest. But she knew herself – never, but never, would she admit her fault, even to a doctor. Fortunately for her, she was lucky that she loved her job, which kept her enormously busy. She would do everything in her power to banish Satan who was stirring up the fire in her soul.

Tatiana was very kind to her, she saw that Victoria was unhappy and tried to reason with her, telling her that no man deserved to have tears shed over him. She introduced her new husband to her! Yes, indeed! After only a month, Tatiana had succeeded in slipping the ring onto her finger! It was record! She had played her cards right, like a real pro! When the heart is serene, it can carry out the most impossible missions...

When Tatiana invited her round to have dinner at their place and present her husband, Victoria was pleasantly surprised by him. He was a very frank boy, who openly said what he thought. He was thirty-two years old, medium in height, brown hair with brown eyes, an open face, and friendly manner. He seemed to be at ease with himself. Before meeting Tatiana, he'd never had time to go clubbing, meet people, and find the right woman. His work demanded all of his attention. Now, he was happy and he wanted to have children.

This young macho had managed, despite his clairvoyance, to be fooled by Tatiana... With his well-bred appearance, elegant manners, and courtesy, Tatiana knew straight away who she was dealing with. She moved into his place three days later, with her suitcases. Patrick was not altogether duped concerning his wife's past, he had made her telephone New York, in his presence, to tell her American friend that she was breaking things off and was getting married. And then she passed him on to Patrick. They had talked. She resumed her studies. So, he asked no further questions, happy about the miracle that was happening to him. But she had at least succeeded in getting him to move from his studio to a bigger apartment! Of course, Patrick's parents knew nothing about this marriage! For this wealthy French bourgeois family, a girl arriving from Eastern Europe was automatically a call-girl. Since her wedding, Tatiana had suffered because of that!   But Victoria imagined that she was concealing the truth, that her Russian dictator still lurked in the background. There was no such thing as perfect happiness. Fiona, her closest friend, was still in love, after more than three years, with a boy who lived in Italy. She saw him from time to time, on weekends, but he couldn't make up his mind to marry her, and she waited and waited... Caroline, another friend, was engaged to a Swiss man. When in Paris for her work, she had met François and fallen head over heels in love. How was she going to confess this and break off her engagement? All around Victoria, the chain of love was not simple. One always desired what one didn't have, eternally starting over again and again...

Cruel split

Victoria was fed up and tired. That very day, just at the end of a fashion show, she had a dizzy spell. The directress of her agency had immediately made an appointment with a doctor. She found that Victoria looked pale and thin. When she went to see the doctor, anxiety and fear came over her. That last night she had spent with Alex, in the heat of their lovemaking... In short, the condom was pierced... And if...? In the waiting room, a host of questions jostled in her head. Until then, she had preferred to avoid tormenting her mind with them.

The doctor ushered her into his office, and asked her all the usual questions for an initial appointment. He asked her the date of her last period. After having examined her, he announced:

"My dear child, you're probably pregnant. You will go have a blood test to confirm my diagnosis, along with an ultrasound scan. Do you know of a laboratory?"

"No..."

"Well, my secretary will take care of your appointments. She will also arrange another appointment with me, so that we can go over the results."

She looked at the medical practitioner in a daze – a stupefaction that was impossible to describe. Her face, as she received the news, nevertheless expressed an unnatural calm. She resigned herself tranquilly to the irrevocable, while a bomb went off in her heart. The truth came like a slap in the face. The secretary gave her the addresses and arranged another appointment. Like a zombie, Victoria left the office. Her head buzzed and she had trouble locating her car. Everything swayed about her.

Back at her apartment, she broke down in tears, plunged into an almost bottomless state of despair. The shadow of the apocalypse hovered over her broken heart. She had reaped the seed of their passion! Lying on her bed, she was overcome with dizziness. Since her brother had left, she had kept mostly to herself. Her girlfriends didn't understand, but respected her silence. They thought that Victoria had simply broken off an unhappy affair. If they only knew... What would she do? What would become of her? She only saw one solution, obviously: an abortion. At this idea, she felt sick. She went to the bathroom, removed her makeup and spent some time brushing her long auburn hair. The mirror reflected the extreme pallor of her face. After taking a bath, she dressed in a ivory-colored satin dressing gown. Her head was empty and her gestures became mechanical. She tidied her bedroom, and left a message for Bernard on his answering machine, telling him goodbye. She wrote a short note to Alex, asking him to forgive her act, but she no longer had any desire to live. This way, no one would pierce her mystery. Then she went to sleep.

Bernard queried his answering service for messages, as he usually did. He was dumbfounded when he heard Victoria's message. She had a voice from beyond the grave. Without wasting any time, he asked directory assistance for the number of the *concierge* at Victoria's building. Did she have copies of the keys? He called her and explained the situation. Luckily, she had the keys. The poor woman was beside herself with panic.

"Call the emergency medical services, I'll be right over!"

Caught in traffic jams, he had difficulty controlling his nerves. He called Victoria on the telephone, but got her answering machine instead. He did not know the time of her call, because he had not downloaded the message from home. He had a lump in his throat. He'd noticed her suffering, but he had not thought she would reach this extremity. His heart was leaping in his chest. When he arrived, the *concierge* there, looking very pale, but she reassured him. Thanks to him, Victoria had been saved in time. The pills had not begun to work, she had only just taken them. By pure luck, Bernard had received her message a few seconds after she left it. It wasn't her time. She'd been transported to hospital for a stomach pump.

Bernard went to the hospital to see her. When he entered her room, she was asleep. Her Madonna's face, extremely pale, contrasted with her flamboyant long hair, spread out on the pillow in long waves. She seemed so fragile, so unreal that he was deeply moved. A rage shook him, a murderous impulse towards the unknown person responsible for the this ill-considered gesture. He approached the bed, leaned over her, and deposited a kiss on her cheek. Victoria slowly opened her eyes.

"Bernard..."

"Yes, it's me, Victoria."

He took her hand, it was like ice.

"Why did you do it, Victoria? Did you think of Alex? He has only you in the world!"

"Promise me not to say anything to him."

"I promise. You gave me the biggest scare of my life! Never do that again, do you promise? I want you to know I'm here day and night for you and will help you no matter what the circumstances."

He kissed her hand and held it in his to warm it. His words and his presence comforted Victoria. Bernard left the room, after making sure that she had fallen back to sleep.

The next day he went back to the hospital to fetch Victoria home. The doctor on duty advised him not to leave her alone that night. A few minutes after they arrived at her place, the phone rang. Victoria signaled to Bernard that he should answer.

"Hello?"

There was a suave voice at the other end of the line:

"Is Victoria there?"

"Who's calling?"

Bernard raised the volume so that Victoria could hear:

"Tatiana."

Bernard gave Victoria a questioning look. She acquiesced with a flutter of her eyelids.

"Victoria had a fainting spell two days ago. I am a friend."

"A fainting spell? Nothing serious, I hope? May I speak to her?"

"That is to say... she's very weak."

"So it is serious! May I come round to see her? I have nothing planned this evening, I can stay with her."

Victoria nodded her head.

"Yes, come."

Tatiana guessed that Victoria had attempted suicide. She had been unwell recently, overly anxious and preoccupied. Tatiana had also gone through something similar, she knew what it was like. Victoria had no family, except for her brother who was on the other side of the world. Her friend Fiona was in Italy. How fortunate that she had called! She'd wanted news since the dizziness at the show. Overwork, she had thought.

"Are you her friend?"

"I'm a friend of her brother's."

"Ah!" she said in a relieved tone.

She went to the bedroom to see Victoria. She had become very attached to her. Since their first meeting, Victoria had never judged her and always been adorable towards her. This evening, she felt all the more close to her because she understood her suffering. She leaned over the bed and kissed her.

"I'll stay with you this evening, all right? Patrick is in London."

That was false, but that way, Victoria would feel less awkward. Bernard and Tatiana withdrew from the room to let her get some rest. In the living room, Tatiana asked Bernard questions:

"Do you know what happened?"

"I don't know any more than you!"

"Have you known Victoria for a long time?"

"No, I met her just recently. I'm a friend of her brother's."

"Are you going to let him know?"

"No, of course not. I'm terribly worried about her, it happened so suddenly!"

"She had a dizzy spell the day before yesterday after the show. That was the reason I called, I wanted to see how she was feeling."

Bernard refrained from telling her that Victoria had left her a message on his answering machine. Indeed, why had she called? Yes, why him? They barely knew each other, they weren't intimate... Was it perhaps because he was the friend of her brother, so that he could let him know in case of a tragedy? Yes, it was surely that.

Tatiana asked him, "If you're not busy this evening, stay for dinner with us."

"With pleasure."

Tatiana went into the kitchen, and Bernard followed. She opened the refrigerator and the cupboards to find out their contents. Apparently, there wasn't much there with which to fix dinner.

"I'll go down to do some shopping. I'll buy what's needed to make her some vegetable soup. That will do her good."

"Stay close to her, I'll take care of the shopping," Bernard suggested.

"As you like..." said Tatiana, agreeably surprised by Bernard's reaction.

He returned a half hour later, his arms loaded with provisions. He'd bought ingredients to make soup for Victoria, but he'd also been to the Lebanese takeaway.

"Victoria likes to go to there: you never know, she might feel hungry...

Victoria refused to even taste her soup. In her state, she couldn't swallow anything.

"Eat a little, Victoria, it will do you good. Humor me, try my soup. Do you know what Bernard bought for the meal this evening? Lebanese dishes! He said you liked their cooking, is it true?"

Victoria smiled weakly: wonderful Bernard, he was so attentive. Although she was in a somewhat comatose state, Victoria guessed from her friend's excited mood that she'd fallen under the enchanted spell of the dark, handsome man. That was all she needed! She finally fell into a deep sleep, disrupted by an erotic dream:

She was lounging back, eyes half-closed, in a bubble bath. Alex arrived, leaned over her face, and kissed her on the lips. Surprised, she wanted to react, but their two faces sank into the sudsy water... She felt herself choke. Alex lifted her face out of the water, smiling at seeing her momentary panic. His handsome nude body stepped into the tub to join her in the bath. She tried to push him away, but weakened under his caresses... Now, it was she who found herself lying on top of him; the contact of their skin, the coming-and-going of their bodies covered in suds, and their words of love carried them to seventh heaven...

Victoria woke up, still pervaded by this scene... It took her several minutes to realize that it was only a dream. Disappointed, she buried her head in the pillow to stifle her sobbing. Even in her sleep, he came to torture her. She looked at the time; it was nine o'clock in the morning; a smell of toasted bread filled her room. She remembered, all of a sudden... Her act, Tatiana, Bernard... She shivered despite the warmth of the room. She put on a dressing gown to go to the kitchen, but everything swayed around her and she just had time to lay back down on her bed. She made a sound knocking over a glass that was sitting on the bedside table. Tatiana came running in, worried.

"Victoria, are you awake? You frightened me! Did you hurt yourself?" she said, seeing the broken fragments of glass.

"No, I made a false move because I felt dizzy."

"That's normal, you're still weak, especially since you didn't eat anything yesterday evening," she said, gathering up the glass debris. "Would you like some tea?"

"Yes, I would like some."

Tatiana came back several minutes later, with a well-stocked tray: toasts, croissants, jams, honey, and orange juice. Victoria looked at her, surprised and touched.

"You really are a great girl!"

"You should be thanking Bernard, it's he who brought the croissants and the rest. He took care of everything, even me!"

"Ah?..."

Victoria remained speechless. As she buttered some toast, Tatiana recounted the evening:

"We talked until five o'clock in the morning! He's a fantastic guy! When I saw how late it was, I proposed that he sleep on the sofa, but he refused. He said he'd drop off the croissants in front of your door about 8:30. I got up a little earlier, but he'd already come by, so I couldn't thank him..."

"In front of the door? How did he get in, since he doesn't have the building code?"

"He must have asked for it from the *concierge*. Yesterday, when you were sleeping, she came upstairs to see how you were. She's very helpful. She told us that, if we needed her, we shouldn't hesitate to call her. For you, she's available night and day. She likes you a lot! But who wouldn't like you? You're so nice, everyone melts in front of you. Me first of all!"

Victoria thought of her Alex, who had been so present throughout the night. Why did he have to wander through her nights and disturb her sleep with erotic scenes? She already found it so hard to forget about him during the day. She felt like she was suffocating and pressed her hand against her throat to help herself breathe. Tatiana observed that her friend was not at all well.

"What's wrong, Victoria, are you ill?" she asked, worried. "Do you want me to call the doctor?"

"No, it will go away. It's just nervous."

"I'll let you rest. I'm boring you with my chatter."

"No, on the contrary, stay here next to me, I don't want to be alone with my thoughts. Tell me, did you let Bernard know you were married?"

"Yes..."

"Do you like him?"

"Up to now, I've never met a man I liked as much as him! Life is so awkward! I've fallen for a man who won't even look at me!"

And for a very good reason! He's in love with my brother!, Victoria thought bitterly. But she refrained from make any comment, it was not her secret. Her own was already heavy enough to bear. Tatiana, seeing that Victoria was interested in her story, became carried away. She asked her if she thought she might have a small chance with him.

"He must be a good lover, I'm sure of it," Tatiana continued. "There are signs that don't lie. There's a force, a virility, and a sensuality that emanate from him. I want to curl up in his arms, kiss him..."

She was in a frenzy! Where were the fine words, the advice, and the teachings of Madame Liouba? Apparently, they'd flown in the wind!

"It's awful, I'm feeling terrible, and I want to cry. It's a bad sign."

"But you barely know him! You'd better snap out of it before it's too late!"

"It's already too late! We talked all night. We have tastes in common, the same way of thinking."

"That would surprise me very much..." Victoria couldn't help herself from saying.

"What do you mean by that?"

"Your way of conceiving life and your behavior with men! Beware of love! It's trying to trap you, and believe me, it can do you a great deal of harm."

"Why are you telling me this?"

"To put you on your guard. The experience that I'm going through is making me ill. I'd give anything in the world to go back to square one and not do anything irreparable. If I have any advice to give you right now, it would be to remind you of that fine phrase you repeat so often: 'To reign, you must keep a cool head.' If you taste this elixir with him, you're sunk. I've never tried drugs, but I'm sure that this must have the same effect. Being without the man I love is unbearable, it's for that reason I wanted to die. He's in all the pores of my skin... This love is wearing me out, it's emptying me, and paralyzing me. I'm losing my reason!"

Tatiana had goose bumps and her eyes stung. There was so much suffering in those words!

"Is there no hope? Even if he's married?"

"Absolutely none, that's my tragedy."

She couldn't reveal the truth to Tatiana. Her reaction was immediate:

"You've run into a lout!"

"It's all my fault, I should have trusted my intuition. There are two categories of men: men and monsters. He was a monster, I knew it from the very start and now I'm paying the bill today!

"Why a monster?"

"Because he makes love without feeling."

"So, I'm a monster, then?"

"It's valid for women, too," said Victoria, smiling. "That's the reason you're badly placed to judge my ex-boyfriend!"

Seeing Victoria's pallor, Tatiana suggested:

"You should take a few days off to rest, it would do you the greatest of good. What do you think?"

"Well, I really don't feel I'm strong enough to start working again right away. That's all right, my agent hasn't anything programmed for me in the coming days. It's true, I do need to rest and take my mind off things."

"If you like, I can get free and leave for a few days with you by the seashore. Deauville, for example: it's not far and the air is invigorating. At this time of year it's peaceful. We'll take beautiful walks by the sea, do some thalassotherapy. There's lots of entertaining things there to occupy our time! We'll have plenty of choices. Patrick has to leave again on a trip for business; if he knows that I'm leaving with you, I'm sure he'll accept it."

"Why not? That's an excellent idea. I adore Deauville, but I prefer Cabourg in this season, it's more romantic. The Grand Hôtel, facing the sea, is magnificent, saturated with memories... It was Marcel Proust's favorite place, he was inspired by it. To think that his first manuscript was rejected by a considerable number of editors before it was published. Today, his talent lives through the centuries!" said Victoria pensively.

"I don't think it's the ideal place for your morale. You need a place that's more tonic! That's why I thought of Deauville."

"You're right

Victoria was completely anesthetized by her suffering. The tranquilizers had their effect. She was despondent and no desire enthused her. To please Tatiana she pretended to have recovered her serenity. But it wasn't the case. Tatiana continued:

"If we asked Bernard to accompany us, would he perhaps agree to come with us?"

So that's it!, thought Victoria. Without further delay, Tatiana called her husband:

"Darling, I'm still at Victoria's. Yes, yes, she's much better. She had food poisoning. I'm coming home, call me in an hour. I kiss you. Hear from you soon."

She hung up, thoughtful.

"He's too nice, my husband; sometimes I'd like him to react more severely to my attitudes. I cry, I scream, at the drop of a hat. But he's always there, willing to satisfy my whims. I would like a man, a real one! Like Bernard."

If she only knew!

"If I understand rightly, you're a masochist, you like rough love? Or impossible love?" said Victoria.

"Neither the one nor the other. I would like to know love, real love, with its passions, tumults, and follies. Not this daily purring where nothing happens, where everything is flat, calm, and dreadfully bleak. I want a love that changes your life, your mood, that makes your soul quiver, that makes your body crazy with pleasure and desire, that makes you mad to the point of losing your identity. For that kind of love, I would exist, I would even sell my soul to the Devil! I'd go to the end of the world to meet it."

"You don't know what you're saying," responded Victoria, horrified. "Your husband is marvelous; in your shoes, I'd do anything to keep him. Men like him, believe me, are hard to find these days. According to

Fiona's aunt, who's a gynecologist, 80% of her patients confess that their husbands are bisexual! As far as sexual relations of married couples are concerned, they fail to meet expectations. Always the same gestures before going to sleep: they set the alarm, make love in five minutes, if you can call that 'love'... and fall asleep leaving their wife unsatisfied... Not a very joyful program – I would even say: disappointing. Happily, there remains the other 20%! You should realize how lucky you are and not do anything stupid you may bitterly regret one day. Mad passionate love only brings suffering and torture when it's a one-way street."

But Tatiana wasn't listening to her, she was lost in her own thoughts. Bernard had enthralled her, she wanted to see him again and hear his voice. She took leave of Victoria, after making sure she didn't need anything. Apparently, if Victoria spoke in this manner today, it was because she controlled her situation more than yesterday. Victoria herself reassured her on that point:

"You're right: let's leave, I need to rest, I've been too overworked lately. I'm going to pull myself together and rebuild my health. Promise me not to say anything to anyone."

"I promise you."

Once she was down in the street, Tatiana had only one desire: to hear Bernard's voice. Victoria's advice and her example had a contrary effect on her. It excited her to meet love and to play with it. It gave her energy and vigor. She had never known a sentiment this strong, that perturbed her to this point! She took out the visiting card he had given her and tapped his number on her cell phone.

"Hello?"

At the sound of his voice, she trembled with emotion.

"Hello? Bernard? It's Tatiana. I'm not disturbing you, I hope? I'm calling you as we agreed."

"Thank you. How is she?

"She's much better. She seems calm, I would even say serene, as if nothing had happened!

"So much the better! I prefer that! She scared me so badly!"

"Me, too. I advised her even so to take a few days' holiday. I proposed to go with her, so she would not find herself all alone."

"She accepted?"

"She didn't say no to me. It would be great if you could go with us, it would please Victoria," she told him straight out.

There was a silence in her receiver.

"Hello? Bernard, do you hear me?"

"Yes, I hear you. I'm thinking. I think your idea is excellent. I'll see if I can get free for a few days. We'll call one another. Bye, Tatiana."

In her excitement, she'd cut off the call. People were staring at her curiously. She realized that she was squatting against a plane tree in the avenue, her bag in front of her. She hadn't even been aware her position was uncomfortable and not very esthetic. But she couldn't care less.

"Wow!" she yelled after she'd hung up.

She went gaily to the nearest Metro station. In her head she was preparing all sorts of scenarios to seduce Bernard. It was lucky for her that he wasn't in love with Victoria. She thought only of him, his face danced before her: he had beautiful eyes and lips. She adored his long, fine hands. His voice was like a melody. He had a good figure, a beautiful body... It was amazing how virile he was! She was overwhelmed by him. Arriving home to her apartment, she called Victoria to tell her that she had phoned Bernard and proposed that he come with them to Deauville. Victoria listened to her, stunned. Was her friend losing her reason, too? She had seen Bernard for the first time only a few hours ago and already she was hatching a great scheme, forgetting that she'd only been married a short time. She tried to argue with Tatiana, but the latter was sailing away in her fantasies, to the point that Victoria, faced with her attitude, began to have doubts.

"But, tell me, did you make love with him last night?"

"I would have liked to!"

"Did he make advances?"

"No, alas!"

"Then why all these illusions on his account? Be careful not to break your own heart. I know I'm badly placed to be giving you lessons, but I see to my great astonishment that you're as weak as me. Despite the courses you took at your Madame Liouba's finishing school, you're like all women in love: extremely fragile and vulnerable."

"You're right, I know that. I'm an idiot to raise my hopes, especially since he did nothing to seduce me. Maybe it's that which attracts me to him, this indifference. I'm at a point where I even forgot that I came to your place to cheer you up. It's serious, you see, I'm ashamed of myself."

"You don't have be ashamed, these things happen in life. Your attitude has made me reflect: yesterday I wanted to die, today I want to live in order to..."

"In order to?"

Victoria caught herself in time, and sidetracked her reply:

"It's we who provoke our destiny. Controlling one's passions is the most difficult thing. We believe that we can erase everything and start all over again. We can do that, of course, if we truly desire, it depends on the scale of the damage! It's at the birth of a love that we must be careful, to see if this love can be possible and durable. We need to examine the whole situation. If I had done that, I wouldn't be where I am now! But when love puts you under its spell, when it makes you fragrant with its best perfume, when it intoxicates you with its 'I love you's', you don't want to take pencil and paper to check off positive and negative boxes. You couldn't care less about everything, even your own life. There is no more morality, nothing exists except HIM!"

"You love him that much?"

"Even more! That's the reason why I put you on your guard, knowing full well that you'll do exactly as you please. I have to leave you, Tatiana, there's another call; thanks for last night, you were truly a love. We'll call one another."

She took the other call.

"Hello?"

"Vic, my love, my angel, it's me."

Victoria was dumbstruck, as if she was mummified, no sound came out of her lips. Through an inexplicable reflex, she cut off the communication. The emotion was too strong, she had to regain control of herself. She left the phone off the hook and went to the kitchen to drink a glass of water. She had trouble remaining standing and trembled from her head to her toes. Hearing his beautiful voice had moved the very depths of her being. He, too, was unable to forget about her.

She was angry with him, she was starting to hate him for the pain she endured. To be sure, they were both at fault, but he was the more guilty of the two! When she was with Pierre, Alex had always wanted to be the first to offer her the most beautiful flowers on her saint's day or her birthday. He took her out to the best places, nothing was too good for her. He always criticized her friends, finding in them all manner of defects. He was her Prince, as he liked to say since earliest childhood. No man could compete with him, he crushed them all! And here was the result, more than a disaster, a true cataclysm! What was she going to do now? And the child she was carrying, what was she going do with that? She did not have the courage. Would he be normal? At that thought, she felt nauseous and a wind of madness blew in her head. There was no one around her in whom she could confide, except a doctor. She had tried to take her own life, but death hadn't wanted her, it wasn't her time to die. Why had she left a message on Bernard's answering machine? Was it to let Alex know in case of a tragedy, or had she sent out an S.O.S. so that he would come and save her? But what if he hadn't received her message? As she thought of that, sweat began to pearl her brow. She returned to her bedroom to lie down, she didn't feel very well. She reset the phone on the hook, and it began to ring again. She picked up:

"Hello?"

"Hello? Victoria it's Bernard; I wanted to know how you were doing."

"I'm better, thanks. I was ashamed about what happened. Thank you for everything."

"I would like so much to see you happy. What can I do

to return your beautiful smile to you? What would you say to a cruise in the Caribbean? How about a trip to Mauritius? Didn't you tell me you wanted to go there? I would like to take you to the end of the world, to make you forget your tiredness with life. What do you think?"

What would Alex think? She bit her tongue to prevent herself from saying that Alex had just called her.

"I'm very touched by your invitation! You really are a dear, I'm very lucky to have you as a friend. Without your intervention I would no longer be of this world..."

At these words, Bernard turned livid: she could have actually died if he hadn't intervened so quickly. But she was there, very much alive, and he would henceforth take care of her and protect her.

"You should try to forget about that. You are made for life, for love... Many women would love to have just a third of what you possess. You have no right to let yourself slip away into nothingness. You're young, beautiful, intelligent, you have a job that you love, you have no money problems. Look around you, you trigger passions, you have all men at your feet, even me!" he said in a joking tone, to hide the truth.

Upon her lips, words were ready to spring forth, which would freeze the sun itself in a block of ice. Her ordeal, she had provoked it and she must endure it until the very end.

"I can't go off far away from Paris right now. Taking flight won't heal me. Tatiana suggested going to Deauville."

"Indeed, she talked to me about it."

Bernard was embarrassed...

"She wanted all three of us to go... To be frank, I'd rather just the two of us go... She's very nice, but a little intrusive..."

Oh! Men! Victoria jumped to her friend's defense:

"Yesterday evening, Tatiana didn't know what else to do to make herself useful. Both of you were terrific, I will never forget it."

"You know that I'm at your disposal whenever you want, for a trip to the end of the world, or closer to home, at your convenience. I think it would do you a world of good. If you want to take Tatiana, she will be welcome. Your pleasure is my pleasure."

Victoria was amazed! What elegance! What a gentleman!

"I thank you, Bernard. Your invitation goes straight to my heart, I'll think about it."

There was another call on the line.

"I'll let you go, Victoria; if you need me, don't hesitate to call me."

Alex was at the end of the line, his voice nervous:

"What's going on, Vic? I've been trying to reach you for almost an hour and it's always busy! Was it you who hung up?"

When the "Prince" was on the telephone, she had to be immediately available to him!

"Not at all," she answered in an annoyed voice. "When I answered, there was no one on the line."

"I miss you! I don't know if I can hold out here much longer. Last night, I had a horrible nightmare. I saw you lying down in your bedroom, as if dead, there were people around you. There were doctors and nurses. I woke up in a terrible state of anxiety. You're all right, I hope?"

"Everything's wonderful, don't worry about me. Look after yourself. How's life over there? Your work?" she asked in a gentler tone.

"I'm working hard, I don't have time to go out; anyways, it's better that way. I miss you terribly, I'm unable to forget you... Talk to me about you, princess."

"I'm feeling better. I managed to overcome this madness that affected us. I met a wonderful man, he's very kind to me. I think I'm happy again."

There was a silence at the other end of the line.

"I'll no doubt be coming for a few days to Paris..."

"Alex, don't come right now, you're going to upset me, it's too soon. I beg you, this has already been hard enough for me, almost beyond my strength to bear..."

"My love, my beloved... I love you... You're my whole life, my reason for being... I want to see you, to hold you in my arms. You are mine in my body and flesh, Vic, you hear me? Nothing will ever separate us! I don't care about the rest of the world. I'm coming to find you, I can't live without you. Who is this man?"

God! He apparently suffered as much as she did. What would become of them?

"Our love is impossible, it's cursed. Do you hear me? Cursed. Think about me. Don't break my life, our life. We have to forget, it's our only chance of survival. I love you, Alex, I'll never love anyone but you. But I beg you, give me the courage to erase everything. I can only do it if you help me, if you're happy, if not life has no meaning for me and I'll do something irreparable. I don't see any other solution."

Hearing these words Alex realized the harm he was doing. She was so weak, so vulnerable, he knew she was capable of destroying herself.

"Forgive me, that dream upset me, I lost my head. I'm so far away from you; if something happened to you, I wouldn't survive."

"What could happen to me? I'm doing a job that I love. It was only a bad dream. Look out for yourself, Alex. You're all I have in the world. Protect yourself, do you promise me?"

"I'm not crazy, you have no reason to worry on that account. My work, after you, is my only priority at the moment."

Before hanging up, Alex told her that he'd call her the following day.

"Not tomorrow, I'm leaving on a shoot for an ad. It's me who'll call you when I return."

A soul adrift

She hung up, pensive. Hearing the sound of his voice revived burning memories in her. It was strange, that premonitory dream that he'd had. She hadn't spoken to him about Bernard or her suicide attempt: what good would it do? What would his reaction be if he knew she was expecting a child? At that thought she gave a start and put her two hands on her belly. God, what was she to do? In whom could she confide? The doctor who'd seen her the night before had advised her to go see a psychiatrist! He said that it would do her good to undergo psychotherapy. She knew the cause of her illness: so to what end? Although used to hearing all kinds of things, the psychiatrist would be surprised to learn her secret.

The next day, she decided to go out and get some fresh air. She felt stifled at her place. There was a monstrous traffic jam in the Rue Royale. She decided to turn right to take the Rue du Faubourg Saint-Honoré. It was even worse! The cars did not advance. She was swallowing her impatience when she saw an angel materialize out of the crowd. Yes, that was it, an angel, an almost unreal vision: she must be barely nineteen, if that! She had a radiant face and was as beautiful as a Madonna. She seemed supernatural, passing through the crowd with feline grace, light, almost floating... Her gaze was luminous, as if from a distant world. Stuck between two other cars, Victoria tracked her in the rear-view mirror, to see which direction she would take. The cars honked their horns, obliging her to move forward. There wasn't even a place to double park for a few moments. In her vehicle, she fumed with rage. How would she ever find this angel again? It was with her that she wanted to talk, to tell everything, and to ask the question: why had she taken the veil? Her face had been serene, touched by divine grace. Her image was like a call from God. Instead of doing her shopping Victoria turned right onto the Rue de Rivoli, towards Place de la Concorde, the Champs-Elysées, the Etoile, Avenue Marceau, and finally stopped nearby the Chaillot church. When she went inside, she felt good, the heavy silence providing a great sense of peace. The odor of candles, that indefinable perfume that made her recall the time of her childhood, at the Sisters' school, when she went to Mass every Sunday. She sang in the choir, because she liked Arnaud. He was a choirboy... with his navy blue uniform, his white ankle socks, his varnished shoes with straps, and his beret from which his long chestnut curls flowed. She already had her court of admirers, even then! She remembered the day when a boy had followed her in order to annoy her. To escape from him, she had entered the church – which didn't deter her pursuer. She'd hid in the confessional, when the voice of the priest had rung out:

"My child, I'm listening"

"Father, there's a boy who's bothering me..."

The priest went out to scold the little brat, who ran away without any further ado. Like a good girl, she'd confessed her little sins, always the same: disobedience, lies, greed... She obtained the right to absolution and to any number of Hail Mary's and Our Father's... She retained marvelous memories of this period. Often, she left her girlfriends to come pray. She remained for long moments admiring the saints and enjoying the silence. Smelling this odor of peace.

At her first communion, she had dared ask impertinent questions to the priest who taught them the catechism. She still remembered as if it were yesterday the time when she'd declared: "The Holy Virgin is Jewish, isn't she? So Jesus is Jewish, because you're Jewish through your mother!" The priest almost choked. Faced with her insistence, he'd asked her to leave the classroom and to go do a penance in the church. She'd never gotten an answer, but only a severe punishment. Her mother, who had been informed on the eve of such a great day, had smiled instead of scolding her. She had also been taken aback, but was rather proud, really.

After having lit candles, she kneeled to pray. An idea ripened within her. As the minutes went by, her decision took form. She stared intensely at the Virgin, who had always protected her. She left the church feeling transformed. Was that angel who had crossed the street, when she was in complete despair, perhaps a sign from God? Since she could not live this love she felt, and her destiny no longer had any meaning, she would take the necessary steps to enter a convent. But would they accept her, knowing she was pregnant? Surely not! She would have to find out. If they refused, she would hide her transgression. It would be God who decided for her.

Right away she went to her neighborhood bookshop to ask for the book by that prima ballerina who had taken the veil for ten years. She'd seen a television program about her not very long before. The bookshop owner did not have the book in stock and recommended she try a religious bookshop: La Procure. Victoria, without wasting any time, went straight to this famous establishment. It was huge, almost the size of a department store! Incredible! She didn't know there were so many religious books.

Seeing her looking disoriented, an employee approached her.

"How may I be of assistance?"

Victoria told him what she was looking for. Without any hesitation, he led her to the correct section and handed her the book. Victoria looked thoughtfully at the cover. The employee saw that she was perturbed and hesitant.

"Are you looking for anything else?"

"That is to say..." she murmured. "I'm a novelist, and my heroine enters a convent. I would like to have more detailed information, because unfortunately I can't myself enter those places to describe what goes on there. I thought of this nun, who was a prima ballerina before her entry into a convent, because my heroine is a fashion model..."

"I see... There's another book that might also suit you. Follow me."

He headed for another section. Victoria was not very comfortable. He handed her another book.

"This one is more recent."

"Which would be more interesting for my documentation?"

"It's difficult to choose. Both of them are good, and deal with actual lived experiences. The second one goes perhaps a little deeper into the subject. This sister spent twenty years in a convent."

"All right, I'll take both of them. Do you have addresses for people who want to go on a retreat?" she asked.

"Of course."

"I passed a sister on Rue du Faubourg-Saint-Honoré. Is

there a convent around there?

"Yes, at the Saint-Gervais church at Place Saint-Gervais."

Victoria was struck by his extreme kindness, he was taking care of her as if she were the only customer in the shop! His attitude was that of a priest. It seemed like he had guessed her secret.

"My heroine wants to cut herself off from the outside world. Do you think that they accept pregnant girls in a convent?"

He was stunned by this unexpected question. His eyes sought to detect her thoughts, while remaining very circumspect. He was impenetrable when he responded with a smile:

"I don't think that..."

"That's all right, I'll find out. Thank you for your invaluable information."

He watched Victoria walk away, lost in thought. With the two books in her hand she felt calmer. She didn't have the energy to look through the other sections. She saw magnificent bindings, but she was dying to return home and read these two works. After a light meal, she started on the first, giving priority to the account written by the prima ballerina. She read it straight through, then immediately passed on to the second. The two women, despite having taken different paths, were of the same opinion: their passage through the clerical world had been an ordeal in a desert under the rigors of the monastic rules. It was a closed world, woven out of silence and abnegation, a universe of women folded in on themselves. They were the maids of the convent, servants of the Lord, living dead without any love or tenderness in their lives. Mirrors were forbidden, as were personal objects, depending on the constitution of the religious orders. Within a convent, each sister had to make a vow of obedience to the prioress. To obtain even some sewing thread, they required authorization.

"These rules are a voluntary restriction of individual freedom," one of the former sisters admitted. According to their accounts, prison inmates enjoy better food, and even human contact, than the women living in a convent! No more tasty little dishes, croissants, and other morsels... Every day, they wake at 5:55 a.m., regardless of season, a little later on Sundays. Already, the precision of that 5:55 gave Victoria a picture of the mentality of the place... As soon as they wake, one of the writers described, in a wretched cell, furnished with an iron bed and a chair, there are prayers, followed by a brief wash with cold water, with twenty sisters sharing ten faucets... They must imperatively wear the shirt, skirt, bonnet and shawl provided, and wash in common with their eyes lowered. Once a month, according to the order of a written list, they were allowed a bath, for a quarter of an hour, no longer... Each day, they thoroughly scrubbed the floors, hunted for the tiniest speck of dust, and did everything for themselves: plumbing, painting, gardening, etc., all this between prayers. There were no breaks or days of rest. A monthly visit from relatives or friends outside was allowed, on a Sunday afternoon. Both women had taken the veil when they were very young. They were unaware of the program that awaited them. They had not known love, pleasure, or passion – in a word: the best nourishments life has to offer. They were thus frustrated and ill at ease with themselves, all the more so because they could not accept the femininity that simmered inside them. They were both beautiful. One of them, very sensual, had great difficulty bearing the prohibition of her desires. Of course she did, there's no fighting nature!

Had the regulations perhaps evolved by now? Victoria wanted to forget her life and cut herself off from the outside world, because she could never again love a man other than her brother, or put aside the memory of what she had experienced with him. She wanted to live through prayer and the love of God in order to gain pardon for her sin. She wanted God's absolution, and oblivion. It was different way of dying. She ended up falling asleep towards two o'clock in the morning, her two books having exhausted her emotionally. No, really, she hadn't been expecting that. She would think it over tomorrow. In any case, she would ask for more details before shutting herself away in the house of God. Her sleep was plagued by nightmares:

She was dressed as a nun, and her brother was making fun of her, finding her ridiculous this way. He told her that her sacrifice was useless, that their liaison was only a little romance, that she shouldn't dramatize matters, that they were at the dawn of the 21st century, and that times had changed. She should find another lover and return to the normal world. Besides, he loved another woman and he was getting married soon. Their quarrel took place in a bedroom. He was naked to the waist, as insolent as could be, and even accused her of being old-fashioned... Victoria sobbed; as for him, he smiled. He was lying on the bed and had fallen asleep. Drunk with rage, she could no longer control herself. Since he no longer wanted her, no other women would have him. In a gesture of madness, she cut off his head with a sword.

She woke screaming in terror, sobbing, her body trembling with shivers of horror. It took her several long minutes to get over this terrifying dream. It was horrible: his blood had spattered her and his head had rolled to her feet... She wanted to call him, to hear his voice, but there was the difference in time zones. The passing of days had not erased anything, they only aggravated the wound. Her heart burned up day after day from missing him. Outside, through the windows, winter wept, as her frozen soul wept in dread of her future without light. Her mood was morbid, caught in a vicious circle. How roughly her sin mistreated her! The intensity and the grip of this inaccessible love, as well as the baby she carried inside her, gave it enormous force. For this child, she must at all costs overcome her own pain.

It was day of her second appointment with the doctor. The latter confirmed her pregnancy, after having had the results of the ultrasound scan and the blood tests. She was in perfect health, and the baby was two months along. Victoria emerged from this checkup feeling depressed. It was 3:30 p.m. and she hadn't swallowed anything for forty-eight hours, except a tea that morning. She had an attack of bulimia, suddenly feeling as hungry as a wolf. She wasn't far from the Lipp brasserie, which she particularly liked. It was icy cold outside, although happily it was no longer raining as it had that morning. She wanted to eat something hot and filling. She didn't like going to restaurants alone, but at that hour, few people were having lunch. Feeling somewhat haggard, she was crossing Boulevard de Saint-Germain when a car brushed her violently. She tripped and fell hard on the pavement. The taxi driver got out of his car. Worried, he helped her up. He excused himself, but

Victoria reassured him that she had been more frightened than actually hurt. It was her fault, and she would escape with a big bruise on her thigh. She entered the restaurant, still in a state of shock. The manager recognized her, she often came in with Pierre. He received her courteously with a kind word and ordered a waiter to take care of her. He seated her at a good table, handing her the menu with a gentle smile. Victoria asked him if she could still order a hot meal, otherwise she would content herself with a salad.

"We serve until one o'clock in the morning," he replied.

"Then I'll have *petit salé* with lentils and a glass of *beaujolais nouveau*."

She needed a glass of wine to lift her morale, and it was November 19th, the day France greets the arrival of the new *beaujolais* vintage.

"I'm sorry, we don't have *beaujolais nouveau* here!" the waiter replied.

Surprised, she looked at him with an astonished air and asked him:

"Give me a draft beer."

"You have very beautiful eyes!"

Victoria thought she had misheard.

"Pardon me?"

"I know people must say that to you very often, that it isn't very original on my part, but you have sublime eyes and a great smile. In a word, you are very beautiful."

"Thank you."

Victoria smiled. Usually, in this world-famous brasserie the staff were discreet, courteous, and respectful, they knew their place. The clientele of this privileged establishment was made up for the most part of literary people, personalities, celebrities, and regulars. Was it Victoria's youth that triggered this sudden sympathy? His attitude didn't displease her, on the contrary, it relaxed her and amused her at the same time. He was attentive to her needs and made comments full of humor to surprise her, as if he had sensed her distress. He became touching because of it. She left the brasserie, feeling a little numb. That beer and the copious plate of food that she was unused to eating weighed unpleasantly on her stomach. Passing in front of the Café Flore, she heard Pierre's voice calling her:

"Victoria!"

She started: he was standing there in front of her, full of emotion. He was accompanied by a ravishing young brunette. God, running into him was all she needed right now!

"Hello, Pierre."

They kissed.

"This is Aurélie, a friend."

"Hello."

"You are more and more beautiful, Victoria, you're looking well! I'm happy to see you. Come have a drink with us at Deux Magots."

"No, I thank you, but I have an appointment, I'm already very late."

But Pierre did not want to let Victoria leave, too happy that chance had put her in his path. Aurélie seemed uneasy, her look was full of questions. She guessed that Pierre was madly in love with the other girl: he was devouring Victoria with his eyes, to the point of forgetting her presence. He had told her about Victoria, but she hadn't expected to find her so attractive. Victoria was aware of her concern.

"You're very pretty, Pierre has good taste! I have to leave you, because I'm going to be late for my appointment. See you soon, I hope."

She left them hurriedly, melting into the crowd. Pierre remained thoughtful: if he hadn't been with Aurélie, he would have insisted on staying awhile longer with her. He wanted to see her again, he hadn't managed to forget her. He had betrayed her, now he was paying for it. He knew Victoria: she had too much integrity and was too proud to forgive him. He would never again find a woman of her qualities. Aurélie was pleasant, but bland next to what he had known with Victoria, who possessed an instinctive intelligence, and with whom he could converse about anything. She was curious as to philosophy, art, culture, and everything that could elevate the soul. Sensual, romantic, sparkling, and full of humor, she had a strong personality that never did anything halfway. With her, it was all or nothing. A truly passionate woman who had added excitement to life. He loved her body, her skin, her perfume. She vibrated, she burned, she shone. She often prepared intimate dinners by candlelight, taking pleasure in decorating a pretty table and concocting the dishes he liked. She was a marvelous homemaker, despite her demanding job. But she liked to please him.

He arrived at his work feeling exhausted. He was pampered and loved. A dream, what! With Aurélie, it was different. She hated housekeeping and cooking; he only ate frozen food now, and she whines from morning to night! Never content. So much so that he took her almost every night to eat at restaurants in the neighborhood. He didn't ask her to cook all the time, to be sure, but a little effort, if only once a week – Sunday, for example – would have given such pleasure. But that was the day Aurélie recuperated from work and rested. Fortunately, there was a cleaning lady to take care of the rest. It was true that his mother had never worked a day in her life; she'd had the leisure, if one could call it that, to look after her family, and she never stopped. In the evenings, she was worn out. Now, women worked and things were different. They were no longer the servants of the home, but women with responsibilities! Nevertheless, he dreamed of a wife who would stay at home to take care of him, and the children. Like his mother...

"Are you still in love with her?"

Pierre gave a start.

"She's an exceptional girl," he said, avoiding the embarrassing question.

"She doesn't not go unnoticed! You didn't lie to me, I'm starting to understand," she murmured.

Pierre, still lost in his thoughts, did not hear the end of her sentence. Aurélie, like himself, was of the Jewish faith. His mother had been against his union with Victoria, because she was a goy, a Catholic. Jewish mothers are in general very possessive, exclusive, very much like mother hens, especially with their sons. He had to be first in everything. Already, when he was in school, if he was only second in his class, she didn't want to sign his report card! She dreamed that he would become a great professor of medicine. She was full of ambition for him. He preferred to be a lawyer, it was his choice. She was nevertheless proud of his success, but she still treated him as if he were eighteen years old! If he let her, she would come by every day to tidy his apartment, iron his clothing, and cook him the meals that he liked. He had a wonderful mother and an exceptional father. It was a solid couple, who had given him an education with a sense of family, duty, and honor. His mother wished at the bottom of her heart that he marry a girl of the same religion. She was glad he was no longer with Victoria, affirming endlessly that she wasn't the right woman for him. How mistaken she was! Only she made him happy. For his mother, only Jewish girls counted. Victoria had, however, done her utmost to win his mother over. But it was useless. He'd even asked her the question:

"If one day we get married, will you adopt my religion?"

"I've already adopted it since I love you."

"That's not what I mean. Would you convert to Judaism?"

"I need some time to reflect on that, don't you think? I can't answer you now. My religion was transmitted from generation to generation in my family. To renounce it would be... how can I say this to you?... yes, it's this: a betrayal. If I was born in a Jewish family, I would behave the same in relation to a Catholic."

"But when we have children, the question is going to be posed. Children, for us, are Jewish through the mother. My family practices its faith; it's not possible for them that it be otherwise."

"I understand, I'm aware of that, and I respect your religion, but for me it's too grave a decision to answer you lightly. If there exists a solution where I can keep mine while adopting yours, I would say 'yes' right away!" she had answered. "Religion, for me, is like the umbilical cord that links me to the deepest roots of my ancestors."

Now, the question no longer posed itself. Since he had

lost her, Pierre had changed, he had even started to drink to forget his heartache. He went to see a doctor to get a prescription for tranquilizers. The latter had advised him to get hold of himself, go out more, saying that no one was irreplaceable. With willpower, one managed to change things. He might have been of a different opinion if he had known Victoria. He followed his advice, but today he was all messed up after having seen her again.

Her birthday was soon: he would send her flowers. She was very touched by such gestures. To be sure, some flowers would not make her return to him, but one never knows, does one? She looked sad. Had she perhaps had an unhappy love affair? He'd try his luck: nothing ventured, nothing gained. With this idea in mind, he felt himself able to win her back by all possible means.

Arriving back at her place, Victoria was surprised to find nearly a dozen messages on her answering machine. Her friends were worried by her silence. They were there for her in this difficult moment, but they couldn't do anything for her. Before calling them back, she dialed another telephone number, that of the Saint-Gervais convent. A pleasant voice answered her. Victoria told her the motive for her call: she wished to enter the convent in order to cut herself off from the outside world. The sister listened to her attentively, surprised by Victoria's determined tone.

"Contrary to what you're looking for, here we are free. Our mission consists in being available to help people in difficulty, people who are ill. We have a lot to do with the outside world."

"Does there exist a convent in Paris where the sisters are cloistered?"

"Of course! Even in Paris."

"Could I have their addresses and numbers?"

The sister kindly provided her with some addresses. Notably one in Paris, in the 16th *arrondissement*! She had trouble imagining sisters walled up in a thick silence, interrupted only by prayers, right there in the heart of the noisy city! The patience of the sister at the other end incited Victoria to asked if these nuns could be seen.

"Oh, no! You can't approach them or see them."

Victoria insisted: it was very important for her. In view of the dismay she sensed in the her voice, the sister gave her the address and the number of the convent.

"They won't answer or receive you. It's entirely closed. You should send a request via monsignor the bishop. But perhaps you could see them at 6 p.m. at the church, during the service."

"Thank you, my sister. Could I meet you? Talk to you?"

"I don't have much time to devote to you: it isn't part of my mission to provide you information."

"I understand. May I know your name?"

She hesitated.

"Sister Marie-Paule..."

"Thank you, my sister, for these precious details."

Victoria hung up, full of thought. How calm, how serene, that nun seemed! She was the voice of the siren. Victoria promised herself to go see her at the Saint-Gervais convent. She was curious to discover her face. It would be strange if it turned that she was the "angel" Victoria had glimpsed in the Rue du Faubourg Saint-Honoré. Without waiting, she dialed the number of the convent of the Sisters of B. that this nun had given her. The convent that was inaccessible. Victoria was transfixed as she listened to the voice that spoke on the answering machine. It was beautiful, deep, and as sweet as that of Sister Marie-Paule. The voice of a saint who came from another world...

"Be welcome. Pardon us. You are in communication with an answering-recording service. If you wish to leave a message for the nuns, please speak after the signal. Thank you infinitely."

The voice spoke slowly and calmly, in a quiet tone that was as attractive as the song of mermaids. Victoria left her name and number, and requested an interview with the prioress. When she hung up, she felt a strong emotion mixed with a sentiment of panic. In a second, she had become conscious of the gravity of the step she was taking. Everything was shaking inside her, it was as if she was being sucked into a spiral that she couldn't describe. Her whole world was spinning round her. Tomorrow morning, would she receive a call? How would she announce to her brother and her friends that she wanted to enter a convent? They would think she'd gone mad. But who cared what they would think; she wouldn't tell them anything before being sure of her admission. Her decision had been taken: she would make an appointment with the mother superior in a convent close to Paris.

The phone rang: it was Bernard asking for news of her. He announced that he had to leave for New York the following morning and would be gone ten days, that he would call her upon his return. She returned the calls from her girlfriends: Fiona, Tatiana, and the others. They all wanted to dine or lunch with her. But Victoria invented excuses in order not to offend them. She wanted to be alone, to meditate; she was too perturbed to go out, and she did not wish to give herself away by behaving in an unusual manner. She had changed, she no long had any desires, her heart was suspended in the void. She missed him. Unable to sleep, she turned on the television to take her mind off the subject.

By accident, she came across a program concerning priests in contemporary society. Intrigued, she listened to the debate attentively. It was too bad that she had started watching in the middle, because the subject was extremely interesting. The priests were dressed just like any average person and the youngest among them even looked very trendy! One of them had an impeccable haircut viewed from face-on, but was graced with a smart and very discreet pony-tail behind. He was superb: he had the handsome face of a romantic playboy and the physique of a young male lead. She imagined him very well in tight-fitting pants, a ruffled shirt with puffed sleeves, and a sword in hand as he fought a duel for his belle... Or let loose in a convent full of ravishing novices. With his charm, he'd make all of them fall for him! He would be the Devil disguised as a handsome prince... With a single spark of his seductive and slightly saucy gaze he would relight the fire of their femininity that had been swallowed up by their heavy, homespun dresses. Just think of the damage he would wreak! The convent would be transformed into veritable nursery! Especially since he confessed, with sincerity and humility, that he was not indifferent to pretty women... when the presenter of the program asked him a question about the vow of chastity he had pronounced. Self-assured and relaxed, he replied with intelligence and humor, drawing general sympathy. He was a rock musician, he loved to sing and do concerts. It was stupefying! She thought he was great. He was a modern priest, who had come to terms with himself as such. Why not? The Church had to evolve with the times.

They weren't supermen that could resist the call of the flesh. Another priest, to avoid having sexual desires, practiced intensive sports, notably indoor cycling... What would he do when he was a few years older, and couldn't pedal so fast? Moreover – strangely enough – they showed him in his cell, in the company of another young priest like himself, surfing on Internet. In big letters, there appeared on the screen the Web page they were looking for : an ad about legal unions between homosexual partners! Incredible! The cameraman passed very quickly, but Victoria had time to see it, and to notice a certain twinkle in their eyes... The others looked much more the part they played. But one of them had succumbed to the love of a very young and ravishing parishioner who'd made him lose his head... and his priestly frock. For three years, they hid their liaison, but then he broke down and they married; he became the father of a cute little boy.

When Victoria was a little girl, she believed that the priests who preached to her were chaste and pure as diamond. But the latest news proved the opposite to be the case. On the other hand, as far as nuns were concerned, she was sure things were different. A women wasn't the same, sexually. Although... A former novice present on this same program confessed both her homosexuality and her penchant for alcohol, while declaring publicly that she had bad memories of her time in the monastic milieu, giving some fairly stinging details. The program certainly wasn't boring!

She adored watching it, it was very instructive for her to

discover the reverse side of the coin. "Let he who has not sinned throw the first stone", as Jesus had said.

Before going to sleep, she addressed a prayer to the Virgin Mary, begging her to help and to give her courage. She finally slept after swallowing a sleeping pill. She woke up about five o'clock in the morning with atrocious pains in her stomach. She tried to resist them, but they became more and more violent. She must have had food poisoning. She wanted to get up and take a pill to calm the pain, but she felt a warm dampness underneath her rear, her sheet was covered in blood! She panicked and tried to call the emergency medical services, but her hands trembled so badly that she was obliged to redial the number several times. She was bathed in sweat, shivering, and her teeth chattered. Given the time of night, she didn't dare disturb either Fiona or Tatiana. She became aware of her solitude. If her mother were there, next to her... She burst into sobs. The doctor arrived within minutes of her call. He pronounced a miscarriage. She couldn't remain alone in this state. She had to be hospitalized for forty-eight hours, so that someone could watch over her and provide treatment. He called an ambulance. When she found herself at the clinic, Victoria was immediately taken in hand by the doctor on duty.

The child of love – and of shame – would never see the light of day. She didn't know if she should be glad or grieving. What would have been the destiny of this poor innocent, since she wanted to enter a religious order? She had desired to keep it near her, had thought of actually trying to hide her pregnancy. Face with a *fait accompli*, it would have been difficult for the nuns to force her to abandon it...

She realized a few days later, after her hospitalization, that she was quite mad. Indeed, she telephoned, right after she left the clinic, the Carmelite order of Montmartre, because the Sisters of B.'s convent had not responded to her request. A nasal voice, not that of a young person, answered her call:

"Hello?"

"*Bonjour!* I would like to speak with the prioress, please?"

"What about?"

"I desire to take the veil; I would like an interview with her, so that she can orient me in the right direction."

"Hold the line."

Only a few seconds had gone by when a terse voice came on the line:

"What can I do for you?"

Victoria, without backing down, repeated her demand, astonished to be able to obtain information by telephone.

"One does not enter a convent on an impulse. And not because of an emotional disappointment nor because one is unemployed. It takes a year, even two years, before being accepted in our community! We carry out an investigation beforehand: we have to see you regularly and judge your motivations. Well, I must hang up now, I'm late for Holy Communion. Goodbye."

Without further ado, she hung up. Victoria felt as if she'd been slapped! The woman could not have been more blunt. In the space of a few seconds, Victoria had been put in the picture. The voice had been hard and curt, enough to give her shivers down her spine and to take away any desire of entering that sort of hell. The prioress must rule her poor nuns with an iron hand. She understood that it would not be within that community that she would be able to resurface! They wanted young girls who were healthy in mind and spirit, very robust ones who could carry out the heavy chores. They weren't tender-hearted, as she found out. They would never accept her if they knew the truth! For them, she was inhabited by Satan. It was unhappily the truth. She was not motivated just then to pursue her demand, if she had to lie and tell them she had heard the call of God. At this moment, she lacked strength and she was drowning. She had prayed to the Virgin, and the very night of her prayer, the embryo had become detached. God is great, God is good, He would not have wanted this additional torment to weigh down her life. Unless it had been the doing of the Holy Virgin who had protected her since childhood? This child never could have been happy with the remorse of its mother and the weight of the mortal sin that she had committed. It would have carried this burden its whole life. It was also highly probable, that it would have been born abnormal. No one had found out, not even Alex; she would carry her secret to her grave.

Having lost the child had given her a great shock; she felt herself sinking into a deep abyss, all the more so because she'd told no one of her hospitalization. The secret was a heavy burden to carry. She had to go back to work soon: would it help her get through this violent tornado that was turning her life upside down?

In fact, she could not remain alone any longer with her thoughts. She was suffocating in her suffering. She felt madness was taking hold of her. She had to react before she collapsed into nothingness. Her decision was made. She picked up the telephone and called Tatiana:

"Hello, Tatiana?"

"Victoria! How strange! I was just about to telephone

you to ask you if you were still interested in going for a few days to Deauville."

"That's the reason for my call! Thought transmission really exists, you see?"

"When would you like to leave?"

"As soon as possible: I need to breathe in nature, the wind on the shore, see the ocean, walk along the beach..."

"If you are free, we can leave tomorrow, Tuesday, and come back Sunday afternoon. Patrick is away on a trip, he comes back Monday evening, and I don't have any shows planned this week."

"That's great, me neither! I'll reserve rooms at the Hôtel Royal; at this time of year, there shouldn't be a problem."

"What time will you pick me up?"

"About eleven o'clock. That way, we'll drive peacefully, and arrive in time for lunch. Hmm! I want shrimp, *moules marinières*, and to breathe the sea air while drink a good little bottle of white wine," said Victoria.

"I'm going on a diet of grilled fish," Tatiana said. "I can't wait to be there! It will do us a whole lot of good."

"We're going to restore ourselves to health! All right, kisses, and I'll see you tomorrow.

"Till tomorrow!"

The perfumes of life

Deauville intoxicated her. Early in the morning, they went jogging on the beach. Then they went for a walk. They went for lunch at Honfleur, and they adored shopping in the antique shops.

Victoria showed Cabourg to her friend. Tatiana was enthralled by the unreal panorama that offered itself to her eyes, a troubling sea that melted into the sky, that iodine-filled air that lashed their faces... the wild, magnificent beach that stretched as far as the eye could see... In that season, it was incredibly romantic. Victoria would have liked Alex to have been there beside her at that moment, to enjoy it and feel the vibrations that perfumed the heart... It was a place just made for lovers... She uttered a long sigh.

"What does that sigh mean?," questioned Tatiana.

"I'm thinking that it's a place where one should come with a loved one, out of season, of course! Like right now."

She added:

"Every year, in the month of June, there's the big Festival of Romantic Cinema in Cabourg. The atmosphere is indescribable! It's fabulous. And the setting lends itself to the event. There are even horse-drawn carriages available for hire by the public. The town is full of flowers and it sparkles. I came here last June with a journalist friend, and I was pleasantly surprised to be plunged into the heart of the cinema world, in the middle of stars rubbing elbows in a convivial fashion."

"Will you take me to it?"

"Why not?"

The days went by with incredible speed. They spent delicious moments together. Tatiana wanted to see and know everything. She didn't leave Victoria any respite, as if she wanted to make her dizzy, so that she'd forget her unhappiness. One couldn't be bored for even a second in Deauville, even out of season. Between golf, tennis, the races, polo, horseback riding... there was enough to keep you busy! Victoria collapsed with fatigue in the evening, but it was a healthy fatigue!

Back in Paris, she felt much better: these few days of vacation had given her new life!

Love sickness

The day of her birthday, she received a sumptuous composition of flowers, with a little note full of love from Pierre. It moved her profoundly – what a shame she was no longer in love with him! Alex had also sent a magnificent basket of flowers. Bernard took her to celebrate at Maxim's, where a big private party was being thrown. Two young people, like magicians, organized dances there, transforming the establishment's dining rooms for a single evening into the trendiest club in Paris. The golden youth of the city came to embellish and add springtime perfume to this restaurant that needed to liberate itself from a somewhat faded winter...
It was 8:30 p.m., and she was fastening her evening gown when the telephone rang. She picked up thinking it was Bernard, but her face went rigid and pale, and she sat down in the armchair in order not to collapse from emotion. It was Alex calling from the other side of the world:
"Vic? Happy birthday!"
"Happy birthday to you, too, Alex."
He asked her if she'd received his flowers. He spoke to her joyously, as if all was well. Apparently, he seemed to have forgotten everything. So much the better.
"So, what exciting thing are you doing tonight? I presume that you'll be celebrating your birthday with your friends, right?"
"Yes. I'm going to celebrate my nineteen years at Maxim's, with a friend, a guy."

There was a sudden silence in the receiver. Alex pulled himself together:

"Nice place. A little old for you, though," he replied in an irritated tone. "Your boyfriend must not be a spring chicken!"

And blam! That was just like her brother!

"You're wrong, he's your age and he's superb. The last few months, they've been organizing parties at Maxim's for young people. There's a crazy kind of ambience there. And you, how are you? Your love life?"

"Everything's OK. I'm doing wonderfully fine. There's a different sort of atmosphere here than in France, but I'm getting used to it. Well, princess, I'll leave you. Have a good night. I kiss you very, very hard."

The click of the phone as he hung up clawed at her heart. What indifference he showed towards her! He must have someone else in his life, she was sure of that. It was normal, their story had no other possible solution. A man was stronger than a woman, less sensitive, and had less romantic illusions. She remained petrified for a few minutes, the sobs rising in her throat. She mustn't cry. What good would it do? He didn't love her any more, she would have to turn this black page. He'd already ruined this evening. Hearing his voice had revived burning memories in her. Despite the warmth of the room, she shivered, nervously twisting her hands. It was a bad sign. If could have guessed for a sole instant that she would be dining with Bernard! Destiny was unpredictable. She was getting ready; anger boiled in her. It was over, she was going to get drunk until she forgot his very name. From tonight onwards, she swore, she would disown her brother! He was hurting her too badly. He tortured her spirit and her flesh, he had soiled her soul. To be sure, she was as much at fault as he was, but she did want to hear of him again until her heart had healed. And for the moment, it was in splinters. God, she felt bad! Pain screamed in her guts, she couldn't stand to suffer this way any longer, it was unbearable. There was no miracle cure for this illness, not even a sedative! She would have to take the whole burden upon herself, find the necessary courage and strength. She envied people who didn't know these pains, like Tatiana. If she didn't snap out of it, she was going to sink into madness, while her brother played the dandy in Singapore!

At 9 p.m. the telephone rang: it was Bernard who informed her he was waiting downstairs for her. She gave herself a douse of her favorite perfume with the vaporizer, a last glance in the mirror, and satisfied with her image, she left to join Bernard, her heart in a whirl.

The party was a great success. The young men were handsome, the girls superb, everyone had fun, and were being friendly. Bernard did not leave her side for a second. He glared at all those who approached her too closely. A good-looking young man found the means of sitting next to her, after having had the delicacy to ask her discreetly if Bernard was her boyfriend. She replied that he was just a good friend. Bernard heard this response and was livid. He observed that she wreaked havoc in men's hearts all around her. Indeed, Victoria hid her spite behind a marvelous smile that remained almost fixed to her lips the whole time; she drank champagne to fog her thoughts. It seemed to work, because all the young wolves came up to her to invite her to dance or to talk to her. As if they were drawn to the light that shone in her face and made her blue eyes sparkle. Victoria, conscious of her success, nevertheless remained seated next to Bernard, facing this wild party crowd. The handsome young man whose name was François danced not far from her, with various girls, each more sublime than the other, who were apparently friends. Victoria was amused at the game of seduction that had started up between them. He danced marvelously well, his attitude betraying a sensuous streak. He was sure of his charm and of the effect he was producing on his court of women, who were competing for his favors. Nevertheless, he could not stop seeking Victoria's eyes; he'd noticed her slightly mocking smile, which put him on edge. He was in the middle of a slow dance with a ravishing brunette with long hair. The music ceased a few seconds before starting another tune; he could not resist, excused himself to the other girl, and headed straight for Victoria. He picked a rose which he found in the table decoration and offered it to her. Then he took two glasses, filled them with champagne, one for him and one for her. The big scene...

"To your beauty!" he said with a dazzling smile.

The pretty brunette glared at him, ready to leap like a panther. Victoria said to him:

"Aren't you forgetting your girlfriend?"

"She's not my girlfriend, she's my sister!"

Victoria gave a start. Bernard was sulking, he wanted to put his fist in the face of this young wolf, but Victoria did not belong to him, he had no rights over him. He had invited her out so she could have fun and forget her broken heart. This evening, she was stunning, he never seen her so bursting with life! Her beauty was breathtaking to behold! Her eyes threw off blue flashes. He did not dare to leave her for even a few minutes, out of fear that she'd disappear on the arms of a handsome young man. But whatever was happening to him? Had he gone mad? He was jealous of all the people who approached her, near or far. He needed to relax, so that she would not perceive his bad mood, or else she'd be disappointed in him. With this idea in mind, he got up; he'd seen some friends in the distance.

Time went by and Bernard did not come back. She profited from the break to go dance with a friend she had just met, a fashion model like herself. The evening ended very late. In the car, Bernard's face was tense, apparently he hadn't enjoyed the party. Victoria pretended not to notice his bad mood. Seeing that he was, she bit her tongue to prevent herself from letting slip a gaffe, such as saying, *If you weren't my brother's boyfriend, my attitude might have been quite different.* But that would have been like exploding a bomb!

The "golden angel"

Victoria became aware that her torment worsened with each passing day. Although she went out in the evenings to lose herself in partying and worked relentlessly, nothing seemed to work: morbid ideas jostled in her head, especially at night. She was tempted to take some pills, go to sleep forever, and suffer no more... Christmas was coming, the streets were lit up; this atmosphere did not suit her morale at all. She had hated the holidays at the end of the year ever since the death of her parents: they brought back to her the wonderful memories of her childhood, when her parents were happy and in love. Joyfully, they'd helped their mother to decorate the apartment, the Christmas tree, and the crèche... Everything breathed the scent of happiness, the joy of living, pine trees, stuffed turkey, and pastries. These odors filled her heart with their fragrance. Her mother hid the toys away in the closets. One day, playing hide-and-seek with a little girlfriend, she discovered the secret trove, and her cry of joy alerted her mother:

"*Maman, maman,* look at all these beautiful Christmas presents!"

Her mother went pale. She'd had such a hard time finding a place where the child would not look. Embarrassed, she mumbled an excuse:

"It's Father Christmas who telephoned me to ask me a favor and keep some presents for him: his sack was too full. He'll be back to fetch them. He'll be disappointed if he sees that you discovered packages that aren't meant for you. He could be less generous with you."

Despite her young age, Victoria had looked skeptical, but faced with her mother's attitude, she had not insisted.

Victoria approached the window. The sky was an intense blue and the pale winter sun incited her to go outside. She had nothing planned for the afternoon. Since her phone call to the convent, she had meditated on the decision she would take. She was attracted despite herself. The voice of the prioress, although curt and discouraging, had stirred up her curiosity. She had told her that they held services at 5 p.m. She spent part of her day tidying up. But, at 4:30 she made up her mind and called a taxi. She gave the driver the address of the convent in Montmartre. He seemed surprised:

"Are you going to the basilica?"

"No, to the convent."

She explained that she wanted to become a journalist and that she had to do a report on the sisters who were cloistered there.

"But they will never authorize you to enter!"

"I know, but they go to vespers at 5:00; I may have a small chance of getting a glimpse of them at that time."

The driver looked at her in the rear-view mirror.

"I know this place, I often take tourists to Montmartre. Are you sure the Mass takes place in the basilica?" he said as they arrived at the place.

He slowed down when they came to the cathedral.

"I don't think the nuns would brave this crowd!"

The parvis was covered with people: tourists, all kinds of vendors, mimes...

"You're right."

"Let's go round the back; I know exactly where the

convent is," he said.

He turned around and took a small street. Then he slowed before a gate, majestic and imposing.

"It's there!"

"Stop here."

She looked attentively through the window she had just lowered. The building was austere and mysterious... She felt a heavy silence. Her heart squeezed in her chest.

"How does one get in there?"

At that very moment, an elderly couple, parachuted there by some miracle, came up and rang the gate's bell. Victoria got precipitously from the car, and told the driver:

"Wait for me!"

She called to the couple, who were astonished:

"Do you have someone from your family inside?"

"My sister is a nun, we've come to pay her a visit," replied the surprised lady.

"May I come in with you?"

"But..."

"I beg you..." Victoria said, her voice full of sadness.

The lady hesitated, her husband remained speechless.

" Will you let me have at least a brief glimpse of the courtyard, at least?"

"I don't have the right!" the elderly woman replied in a more authoritarian tone, having regained her wits.

The gate opened and a black nun appeared. She was wearing a long, brown, homespun dress, with a matching veil; the cornet and the plastron were white. She had on brown sandals with dark, thick woolen socks... Despite this austere dress, she possessed a great beauty, with a sharply chiseled face and the bearing of a queen. Victoria, before such an apparition, stupefied.

Even before the lady who preceded her could utter a word, revealing her status as a curious intruder, Victoria intervened quickly, employing her charm.

"*Bonjour*, my sister. May I attend mass at five o'clock?"

"But there is no mass! Who told you that?"

"I mean to say... It was the prioress who told me to come at five."

"Oh! For the service?"

"Yes, that's it! I meant to say: for vespers..."

"Ah! Very good. If you have her permission, come in!"

The taxi driver had, out of curiosity, gotten out of his vehicle. He was a few meters from her. Victoria searched in her bag and handed him a banknote.

"Keep the change!"

Without waiting any longer, out of fear that the sister would change her mind, she penetrated into the sacred place. The nun closed the heavy gate behind her. Someone drummed on the door, and a man's voice rose:

"*Mademoiselle, mademoiselle!*"

Victoria recognized the taxi driver. The nun, surprised, opened the door. The driver, addressing Victoria from afar, said to her, holding up a pair of sunglasses:

"Are these yours?"

"Yes..."

The sister took Victoria's glasses, looking at the man with astonishment. He was tall, athletic-looking, about thirty years of age. He stared at the sister intently, almost undressing her with his eyes. She began to blush, but maintained eye contact with coquetry, a big smile illuminating her face. Victoria watched this seduction scene, astounded. The sister seemed turned on at seeing a handsome compatriot. He was black like her. She turned towards Victoria to ask her:

"Is he part of your family?"

"No, he's the taxi driver..."

"Ah!" she said, disappointed.

Victoria had not had the reflex to try and please her. Would she perhaps have agreed to let him join her?... Without hesitation, the nun asked the man:

"Where are you from?"

"From Haiti."

"Like me!" she said, joyfully.

The driver saw Victoria looking astonished, and gave her a little playful wink. It was true that the nun was resplendent. A real golden sunbeam! But the latter, regretfully, closed the door slowly, a little too slowly, long enough to capture the image of a mirage and fix in her memory the face of a handsome stranger who had come to trouble her. She addressed Victoria, thoughtful:

"The chapel is down there on the left."

"Thank you, my sister. Could I have a conversation with you? I need to speak to you."

"After vespers."

"May I know your name?"

"I'll tell you after..."

Victoria was surprised to find that events had unfolded with such amazing ease. When she penetrated the chapel, she was struck by its austerity. On each side of the nave, there were rows of chairs with pews, facing an altar. This was a square table covered in a white lace cloth, with two big candlesticks on either end. Against a whitewashed wall was a great crucifix without any other adornment. Missals were provided for the faithful. The chapel was empty, and Victoria sat down in the front row... She noticed on her left a big, ivory-colored net curtain that created a mysterious ambience. A lady entered the place. Victoria turned round and smiled at her, inviting her with a gesture to sit next to her. Her presence reassured her because the atmosphere was strange, empty: there was no soul here and a complete coldness. Neither God, nor Jesus, nor the Virgin Mary were there for Victoria. No breath of love came to warm the chapel.

"Is this the first time you've come here?" asked the lady, who had sat beside her.

"Yes..."

She handed her a missal, indicating to her the pages of the evening prayer. She was very sweet, with a pious air. She had short brown hair, a pleasant face, and must have been about forty years old. She was extremely intrigued by Victoria. The latter, despite the fact that she had tied her hair back severely, wore no makeup, and was dressed soberly, gave off an aura, a strong charisma. Behind the curtain, the sound of footsteps could be heard. Then there was silence. Like on a theater stage, the curtain opened gently; the nuns appeared in rows of two, their eyes fixed on the ground, their hands in their sleeves. They wore the same brown and white uniform as the sister who had greeted her so kindly at the gate, except for the prioress who was in black, with white cornet and plastron, and a novice dressed in white. Victoria did not dare look too closely, for fear of attracting attention to herself. Some of the sisters were visible, others sat behind a partition. The prayers began. The voice of the nuns rose, reciting the service in song. Each of them in turn came to the center of the room, where an oratory sat, to chant a prayer out loud. Victoria, her head leaning over her missal, tried her best to look at their faces. It wasn't easy, because the lady next to her spied on her gestures. She had come to realize that Victoria was not concentrating at all on the prayers, but was rather occupied with observing what was happening around her. In the middle of meditation she saw Victoria look worried, discretely search through her bag, take out her telephone, and turn it off. It was true that, it had started ringing, it would have been a disruptive nuisance...

During this service, there about fifteen sisters in all. She had thought they would be more numerous. When the prayers were over, the curtain closed. She heard the sound of chairs being shifted, then nothing. She looked questioningly at the lady, who smiled at her kindly.

"The service is over," she said.

"What happens now?" she asked.

"Nothing. Either you leave, or you stay for an hour to pray."

She gave a start. An hour! But she was here to pierce the mystery of this place and capture its ambience.

"I'll stay to pray," she said. "And you?"

"Me, too," said the lady, surprised, with a slightly ironical smile.

She handed Victoria another missal. She had noticed that the young woman had trouble following. To her great astonishment, however, she had heard her singing in Latin accurately.

"This missal is more complete."

"Where can I obtain a copy?"

"At La Procure, the bookshop."

The door of the chapel opened. Victoria, curious, turned around. The black nun appeared. She beckoned Victoria to follow her. Victoria got up and took leave of her neighbor:

"Thank you for your kindness."

She left the other woman looking pensive and joined the nun, who handed her a ring of keys.

"Here are the keys. When you leave, lock the doors tight behind you. You can drop them off at the gate."

She showed her a door.

"It's on the second floor, the Marie-Ange room."

With these words, she disappeared. Victoria stood there incredulous, the ring of keys in her hand. She found herself in the convent's courtyard. She looked from right to left, wanting to imbibe the odor of silence. She was in another world. A statue of the Holy Virgin reigned in the middle of the garden. The daylight was fading. She went into the place indicated by the sister, and climbed to the second floor. The banisters were in wood, and superb, as were the doors and windows. There was a smell of wax. The parquet floor was shining with cleanliness. At the landing, there were several doors, then a long hallway. She found the door in question. She knocked, but no one answered. She insisted discreetly, trying the knob... it was locked. She knocked a second time; the voice of the nun reached her:

"You have the key!"

She opened the door: the sister was there, separated from her by a wooden balustrade.

"Sit down," she told Victoria solemnly.

She did, and now Victoria found herself face-to-face with her.

"What can I do for you?" the nun asked with a sweet smile.

Victoria was very impressed. She remembered what she'd read in the book by one of the former nuns. Sobs rose in her throat, and tears pearled in her eyes. She was troubled by the physique of this nun. An interior light seemed to glow in her beautiful golden face. She was haloed by a white, snowy color. An optical illusion, no doubt, in the clearness of the evening. Victoria started to talk in a trembling voice, betraying a febrile state despite the power in her gaze:

"I want to devote myself to the Lord and take the veil like you. I've long reflected on this for months now, and my decision is irrevocable. The life outside does not interest me, it's a perpetual failure for me. I wanted to leave this world voluntarily, but death did not want me, nor did God. I don't have the strength to make a second attempt, the gesture was cowardly, and in our religion it's rejected. I have faith, I know that this is my destiny, and that I should pursue the love of God through prayer."

She didn't dare ask this beautiful "golden angel" what had prompted her to choose this path!

"For another thing, I'm glad that my first interview is with you. I should like to know, if possible, how a day goes by here in the convent.

The nun, fascinated by Victoria, her gentleness, and her sweetness, forgot the rules of silence. She detailed to her with considerable care, like a good pupil reciting a lesson, the daily schedule of her community. Victoria listened to her attentively, intervening at times to ask her more indiscreet questions. To her great astonishment, the sister answered, becoming even voluble. As the minutes passed, the nun relaxed and they were discussing matters like two friends. Victoria profited from this moment to ask her:

"My sister, can I note down this information?"

Joining act to her words, Victoria opened her bag to

search for the pencil and notepaper she had prepared. The nun turned pale, her face went rigid, and fear could be read on her face, doubt, too. She got up with a bound, and looked at Victoria as if she were Satan.

"I beg you, don't take any notes. I don't know what came over me. I don't have the right to reveal what goes inside the monastic enclosure. I've committed a transgression, I must immediately inform the prioress. Was it really her who authorized you to see me?"

"I meant to say..." Victoria contradicted.

What a catastrophe! She wanted to keep her there, tell her that it would remain a secret between them, but she remembered the two books she had read. She refrained from acting. The nun headed in a frightened manner towards a door, leaving Victoria to fume at her own clumsiness. She'd ruined everything! She took advantage of the fact that she was alone to look around her. Everything was tidy and very clean. A big crucifix was the sole adornment. The windows looked on the courtyard, they were superb. The view of the trees diffused an atmosphere of serenity.

A fury in black, like a witch, penetrated into the visitors' room like a hurricane, followed by the "golden angel". Her faded blue eyes darted flames through her glasses, censuring Victoria with her inquisitive gaze. Her mouth, deformed by anger, let white dribble flow at the corners of her thin straight lips. The mother superior, with her hideous face whitened by hate, rushed towards Victoria.

"How did you have the audacity to penetrate in forbidden place? You've committed a sacrilege! How gave you permission to enter here?" she said, her eyes bulging, ready to pounce upon her? "Was it you who telephoned me?"

"Yes, my mother."

"I told you that perhaps I would receive you after January 15th! How dare you disobey me?"

"Perhaps it was God who sent me!" Victoria replied.

The prioress was not touched by these words, quite the opposite! Drunk with rage, she turned to sister and shouted furiously:

"For your fault, I will have you convoked by the diocese."

The sister lowered her head; apparently, this didn't seem to frighten her.

"But it wasn't her fault," Victoria intervened calmly with her angelic gaze. "I lied to her in saying that I had your authorization."

Victoria turned to the black nun.

"I'm truly sorry, my sister. I beg you to forgive me."

"It's nothing, don't worry..." she said with an Olympian calm, smiling gently.

She seemed to be delighted to see Victoria standing her ground with this old cow. Victoria added:

"You should be thanking her. I read two books about the behavior of prioresses and the disciplines of convents, that date from the Middle Ages, it seems. Thanks to this sister, I was going to leave with an entirely different opinion. But you just ruined everything!"

The mother superior wasn't listening to her, she kept repeating:

"How dare you? No one, do you hear me, no one from the outside world is to penetrate here!"

Victoria looked her straight in the eyes and, in her most charming tone, replied:

"I already told you, my mother: it's God who sends me, or perhaps the Holy Virgin!"

With nonchalant, almost theatrical, gestures, Victoria ventured to say, sarcastically:

"I'm an angel sent from Heaven, I entered by miracle in a sacred place! Christmas is coming, perhaps that's why I was guided here by a mysterious force."

The "golden angel" had difficulty stifling a fit of giggles. She was exulting, her eyes betrayed her and sparkled with mischievousness. She seemed to be savoring, by means of a third party, a small personal revenge. No nun here in this place would dare stand up to this dragon with a dry heart. She was a sadist of purest sort! She was missing only the riding crop. The prioress looked at her, stupefied, before uttering threats:

"You won't get away with this, I'm going to lodge a complaint with the diocese against you. Send me your address by the post."

"Why by the post? I can give you my visiting card right away!"

The prioress told her in an icy tone:

"Don't bother. Leave immediately! Leave right away, do you hear me? You will send me everything by the post! I'm going to lodge a complaint against you!" she insisted, as she left the visitors' room.

If the balustrade hadn't separated them, Victoria would have torn off her cornet. Then "golden angel" addressed her. Her voice, to Victoria's great surprise, was cheerful, almost as if they'd been accomplices:

"Don't forget to close the doors behind you!"

Apparently, this story had added a bit of excitement to her life of prayers, where Jesus was her sole universe.

If she thinks I'm going to send her my address, that old fury is sadly mistaken! I'm not a masochist! What a horrible person. She locked the door behind here, and

the light went out, leaving her in the dark. Night had
fallen. The bell of the Montmartre cathedral struck
seven; the sound echoing in the hallway, making the air
vibrate. It was very impressive to find herself within this
convent. She was angry at herself for having spoiled , by
a clumsy gesture, the interview just when it was
becoming really interesting. She saw a light switch and
pressed it, but it wasn't working. Had the prioress
deliberately cut off the electricity to punish her? She
fumbled in the dark, the floor was slippery, and the heels
of her shoes didn't help matters. Where the stairs that
led to the courtyard? Minutes went by, she couldn't find
the exit, and this labyrinth was beginning to worry her.
Fortunately, she had her cell phone with her! The nuns
must be at the refectory. Suddenly, an idea crossed her
mind. She would play a prank on the prioress. She
would deliberately barricade herself inside here.
Towards midnight, she would call the firemen, to tell
them she was trapped inside this convent. What a
scandal! Why the firemen? They're generally good-
looking. Victoria was theatrical and fairly provocative at
times, she liked to surprise people. This prank would be
quite successful in that sense. But she soon abandoned
the idea, she was genuinely afraid of this silence that
pounded against her heart and was beginning to stifle
her in this black fog. Feeling her way, she finally found
the banister of the stairway, then the exit door, and was
relieved to be back again in the courtyard. She pulled the
door shut behind her and tried in vain to lock it. None of
the keys worked. A nasal voice called out to her in the
darkness:
"What are you doing?"
She turned round, perceiving vaguely, across the

courtyard, a shadow that approached with a limp. A sister, very advanced in years, bent in two, her head leaning to the right, and who resembled an evil fairy godmother, came up to her. Seeing her ugliness, Victoria gave a start, and goose bumps chilled her... She had the impression of being in a film... Without becoming flustered, she answered:

"The prioress ordered me to lock the doors behind me."

"Give me the keys, I'll take care of it."

"Thank you, my sister. Where is the way out?"

"Follow me."

Despite her repulsive appearance, she was very kind. She didn't ask her any questions. Victoria suddenly found her less ugly. When the nun opened for her the heavy gate that led out to the street, she thanked her warmly. She emitted a sigh of relief once she was outside. Nervously, she tittered with laughter, recalling to mind the details of her misadventure and the appearance of the prioress. And to think that the woman had appropriated the title of "wife of the Lord"! There was no goodness or generosity in her face. She had fixed to her heart a sign reading "Life forbidden" in red, with big capital letters! How horrible! Brrr... The street was deserted; she quickened her step to reach the Place du Tertre. She crossed three kids on her path and asked them where she could find a taxi. She was still under the shock of the emotions she had experienced.

"We'll accompany you."

All three of them were adorable. They were three brothers. For Victoria, they were three angels fallen from heaven. She appreciated their presence at that moment more than ever. They looked at her in admiration. The oldest said to her:

"You're very beautiful. Are you a fashion model? I've seen you in the magazines, and on television, too."

Victoria smiled.

"When I tell my pals that I talked to you, they won't believe me! Could you give me an autograph?"

"Me, too, me, too!" repeated the two others in chorus.

Victoria searched her bag and pulled out three publicity photos. She scribbled some friendly words on each and kissed them. They were mad with joy.

"Thank you," they said, eyes shining.

Victoria headed for a taxi that had halted. The car started, and the kids' hands waved to her goodbye. She arrived back at her place feeling emotionally drained. Christmas was approaching quickly, the avenues were illuminated, and the stores displayed their riches. For the poor, the lonely, people without family, it must dreadful. These holidays only added to their solitude and sense of lack. Everything swayed inside her and the idea of suicide haunted her mind.

She went to do some shopping for dinner. She chose a Nordic salad and a dessert. She stopped at her florist's to buy her favorite rose, which she nicknamed "chocolate" because of its salmon-pink color with brown highlights. When she entered the store, a customer was hesitating over the choice of flowers he wanted to buy. Minutes went by and he couldn't make up his mind. Victoria called out to the florist, a handsome young man with azure eyes:

"Do you have the "chocolate" roses?"

"Yes, they're right behind you."

"Today, one will be enough."

"I'll let you think it over," said the florist to the hesitant man, "while I serve my lady customer."

He took the rose and wanted to wrap it up.

"No, that's not necessary.

The young man murmured to her softly.

"I offer it to you."

"But..."

Victoria thanked him discreetly, she was embarrassed. The customer approached her, seeing her smell the flower.

"I'm not familiar with that type of rose. Why is it called 'chocolate'?"

"It's me who nicknamed it that, because when it blooms, it takes on a chocolaty color and becomes very beautiful."

The customer turned toward the florist and said:

"Do you still have a lot of these roses?"

"About fifty."

"Good, I'll take them all."

Victoria's eyes widened. She couldn't help envying that woman for this splendid proof of the man's love. He went over to Victoria and asked her:

"Do you think that this will please her?"

"Women are always very touched by gestures of love."

Returning to her apartment she set a pretty table, placing her "chocolate" rose in the center. She poured herself a small glass of vodka, to chase away her black thoughts. It seemed to be working at the end of a few minutes. She ate her meal hungrily, treating herself to *blinis* wrapped in salmon. She plugged in her stereo to put on a Brazilian cassette, sunny music to banish melancholy. She had just finished her chocolate cake, drunk a last swallow of vodka, and her cheeks were warm and hot, when the telephone rang. It was Bernard, calling her from New York. He was prolonging his journey until the beginning of January. He asked her if she wanted to spend the holidays with him. Victoria refused gently. He said he would call again to wish her a happy New Year. *Life is awkward at times*, she couldn't help herself from thinking. *He's a handsome boy - intelligent, generous, and full of humor. A dream, in fact! Unfortunately...* Pensive, she cleared away her dishes when the telephone rang again.

"Hello?"

"Victoria, are you there? What luck. I've had trouble getting hold of you these past few days."

Her friend Maya's voice resounded in the receiver.

"Maya! I'm happy to hear you!"

"If I don't call you, you forget all about me," she said.

"How could I forget you? I've been traveling a lot these last few months. How are you? And your husband?"

"We're doing wonderfully well. We miss you. When are you coming to Palm Beach?"

"I don't know..."

"What are you doing for the holidays?"

"I haven't planned anything."

"So come, then. We're waiting for you. The weather's superb."

The voice of Robert, her husband, came on the line:

"Victoria, *ma flor*, come right away: that's an order!"

His accent made Victoria smile. Maya was French, her husband was American.

"You hear that, Vic? We're waiting for you," Maya repeated. "What are you doing alone in Paris? Especially since Alex telephoned me; I know he's in Singapore."

"But..."

"There's no "buts"! I want to see you. Your childhood friends are here, they arrived from New York for the holidays."

She gave Victoria some names. The temptation grew.

"You are dears: why not? I'll call my travel agency tomorrow, to see if there are still seats on a flight. But in this period of vacations, that would surprise me greatly. I'll call you back after."

Victoria hung up, thoughtful. Why not accept? Maya was her mother's best friend.

As a child, Victoria had spent the Christmas and New Year's holidays with her parents and brother in Palm Beach, at the Breakers Hotel. She had kept marvelous memories from those times. Swimming at Christmas in the transparent, turquoise seas, warmed by the sun. Playing in the hot sand, gathering seashells in the shape of hearts... Listening to the gulls cry joyfully... Watching the dance of the birds in the sky, while the palm trees swayed with the rhythm of the air. It was divine.

The next day, she phoned her travel agency. To her great astonishment, there were flights still available. She booked a seat and reserved her return for January 3rd. This way she could get some perspective on her situation and make the necessary decisions. She called back Maya and confirmed her arrival in Miami on December 22nd at 5:40 p.m., local time. There was, of course, a connecting flight to Palm Beach, but it meant waiting several hours. She preferred an hour's journey by car. Maya noted down all this information.

"A chauffeur will come pick you up in Miami. Bravo, Vic! I'm so happy to be seeing you. You won't regret it, you'll see. The weather's great, it's like summer, and the atmosphere is wild, with the right sort of people. Robert will be thrilled."

When she hung up, Victoria was beside herself with joy,

and delighted with her decision.

Palm Beach

After leaving the airport, the limousine passed through a noisy Miami, where the traffic was indescribable. She was stunned to see so many beautiful trucks on the road, in all kinds of colors, covered in chrome, and gleaming with cleanliness. From the way they drove, all these truck drivers seemed happy, proud of having fulfilled a childhood dream. The traffic had slowed on the highway. It was 7 p.m., and people were returning home.

When they arrived at West Palm Beach, her heart fluttered. So many memories caressed her mind. The decor lay spread before her eyes: gigantic buildings on the edge of the lake rose arrogantly towards the sky. She gazed wistfully at the sumptuous boats resting after day of nautical adventures. The change was radical when they reached Palm Beach! The limousine glided through a dreamlike panorama. Everything was beautiful, luxurious, and paradisiacal: the flowers, the luxuriant vegetation, the palm trees, the houses, the private parks, and the golf courses. And that attractive sea, painted with a palette of greens, bordered by white sand, framed by coconut trees that ran along the road as far as the eye could see, illuminated by a setting sun like a big red ball, left Victoria dazzled.

Just as they arrived, forewarned by a call from the limousine's chauffeur, Maya and Robert came out of the house to greet her.

"*Ma chérie*, what a joy! You're not too tired by this long trip?" Maya inquired.

"No, I'm fine. I'm so happy to be here."

"So much the better, because we're having a big party later."

"Hello, my doll, *ma flor*," Robert exclaimed, doing a very bad imitation of a French accent. "I'm so happy that you accepted our invitation!" he said, kissing her.

Victoria was eager to freshen herself up in the bathroom. But barely had she entered the house when Maya led her to the living room.

"Come see our friends, they came expressly to see you."

"I'd like to go change first."

"No, stay like that, you're just fine as you are."

She exaggerated a little. After those long hours of flight, she needed a good hot bath. Maya brought her to her friends. They were there, smiling, getting up to greet her.

"We have the impression we know you since way back! Maya and Robert have talked so much about you. You're as beautiful as in the photos."

Victoria noticed portraits of celebrities, of friends, and photos of her all over the place!

"What would you like to drink?" asked Robert.

Victoria glanced at the glasses of the other guests. Californian white wine had the place of honor.

"A glass of white wine, like you!" she said, eyes sparkling.

Among the guests, she recognized a couple of Canadian friends, who knew her from when she was eight! Except for Robert and them, there were only Europeans. They had all emigrated to the United States. Apparently, they were thriving here. She had gotten a small idea upon her arrival, seeing the beautiful cars parked in front of the house. Palm Beach is another planet, where the biggest fortunes in the world congregate. One may say that money can't buy happiness, but all these people seemed radiant and joyful.

"What are you thinking about, Victoria?" Robert asked. "I find you very pensive."

"I'm feeling culture shock. I have the impression I'm dreaming."

Maya took her to the bedroom where she'd be staying.

"Go get ready, we have to leave in a half hour. We're invited to a big party."

It was 7:30 p.m. in Palm Beach, 1:30 a.m. in France! The night was going to be long for her.

"But my dress must be wrinkled. I'll have to iron it."

"I've thought of everything."

Indeed, upon entering her room she found, unfolded on the bed, a long black dress, with a matching bag. Victoria was stunned.

"Do you like it?" asked Maya.

"It's sublime," she said, lifting up the dress.

"If it doesn't suit you, come pick another one in my dressing room. Hurry up, you have ten minutes to get ready.

Maya left the room. Victoria hurried into the bathroom to take a shower. She put on some light makeup, lifted her hair into a chignon, and put on Maya's dress. It fit her like a glove. The dress was sexy, but at the same time elegant: a sheath, slit down one side, with a deep décolleté and thin straps. She opened her suitcase to look for shoes that would go with it, then attached round her neck a costume necklace with several rows of black pearls. She put on a cloud of perfume and gave herself a last look in the mirror. And so she was ready. She felt good, already caught up in a whirlwind. Since she had known Maya, it always happened this way.

"Are you ready?" inquired Maya, knocking on the door.
"Yes, come in!"

"You are superb!" she exclaimed. "The dress looks lovely on you. Come quickly, we're going to be late. Our friends send you a kiss, they couldn't wait, they had a dinner party. We'll see them tomorrow for lunch. Here, take this shawl, you might need it.

Marvelous Maya, she thinks of everything. Robert waited patiently before the house, in their white Rolls Royce. To see them looking so handsome, so happy, warmed her heart.

She watched the scenery flash by on the road that ran along the sea bordered with palm trees. The smell of leather in the Rolls and all this luxury went straight to her head

"Oh, it's beautiful! You don't know how lucky you are to live in this place. Riding tranquilly in a Rolls around a heavenly town, where the sun shines all year. Exercising the profession you love, which amply rewards you with the means to live and to profit from the good times that pass by."

What's preventing you from doing the same? Nothing's keeping you in Paris. Come live here. What do you think, Robert?"

"Yes, stay with us. Maya's right: what are you doing alone in Paris?

"It would tempt me to live here, but I can't do without Paris. I have my work, my friends, and my habits."

Paris is a jewel, she thought. How can one live without being surrounded by the spiritual nourishment that lets the soul blossom? Art, culture, philosophy, literature, music. Visiting museums, going to the theater, to the opera, to concerts, to exhibitions... Shopping in antique shops, bookshops, and galleries. Walks in the capital's old neighborhoods, that resemble little villages, where one finds extraordinary people: painters, musicians, poets, writers... Discovering astonishing "Ali Baba" boutiques, and delicious, friendly little restaurants. Going to the flea market on Sunday mornings, lunching to the sound of an accordion. Paris makes hearts beat, and heads turn, it's a magical, inexhaustible city.

Despite the parties, the outings, the sea, the beach, a magnificent Christmas, Victoria was not happy: she still missed her brother as much as ever. The morning of New Year's eve, Maya came to visit her in her room.

"Good morning, Vic. Come have breakfast with me. But what's wrong?" she asked, seeing Victoria's reddened eyes.

Victoria burst into sobs. That night again, Alex had come prowling in her dreams. She confided in Maya, telling her that the man who made her suffer was not free.

"Stop making yourself ill! He isn't worth it. You are young, beautiful, and intelligent, with your whole life before you. Look, the weather is superb! Ideal for going to the beach. This evening is the party, you'll find your friends and celebrate the New Year. It's going to be grand; the setting of Mar Largo is made for it, and Donald Trump always does things well. He's got Donna Summer coming to sing."

She would have to forget her broken heart. The streets of Palm Beach were sparkling, and a festive scent brightened the town. People were smiling and happy. They were getting ready to greet with enthusiasm the year 2000.

When they arrived at Mar Largo, cars, each one more luxurious and gleaming than the next, stopping in front of the entrance, where a team of well-organized bellboys greeted the guests. As Maya predicted, the place was magical. The men and the women were breathtakingly elegant. The decor was unreal. The palm trees that rose into the sky were illuminated in blue, green, and red. The buffets were sumptuous. The orchestras followed one after another. Donna Summer gave a remarkable performance, creating a warm atmosphere. It was a succession of surprises. After the show, Victoria walked in the gardens – it was so romantic. She wanted to flee from this joyous crowd, who only fuelled her nostalgia. She saw him everywhere and was unable to chase away his image. Each piece of music broke her heart. She leaned on a balustrade that overlooked the swimming pool. People were dancing and having fun. She looked with a thoughtful air at the spectacle of this festive crowd. When Donna Summer counted down the final seconds of the year, her heart squeezed painfully. She bit her lower lip while her eyes stung, watching the couples embrace passionately. She thought very hard of her brother, to wish him all the happiness in the world. For herself, she expressed a wish: to forget and to find once again peace in her soul. Her eyes were lost in thought, when:

"Victoria? I'm dreaming, it's not possible!"

She gave a start, and turned round. In the darkness she distinguished three young men, but she couldn't make out their faces. One of them approached her.

"Chris!" she exclaimed. "How I'm happy to see you!"

"What a beauty! What a beauty, my Victoria," he said, taking her into his arms. "Meeting you is the best possible present I could have for the year 2000!"

They kissed, moved at have found one another after so many years.

"I'd like to introduce you to Victoria, a friend from my childhood," he said to his friends with a big smile.

He made the presentations:

"Victoria, these are Steve and Bernard, a friend from Paris."

Both of them stood there for a second, stupefied! Bernard reacted first:

"But what are you doing here? I thought you were in Paris!"

"Friends of my mother invited me, and I accepted. It wasn't planned."

Chris, astonished, intervened:

"You two know one another? What a small world! We're going to celebrate the year 2000 together, that's great!"

He spotted a free table near the dance floor. He took Victoria tenderly by the arm and murmured in her ear:

"Too bad I'm with my friends, I would have liked to be alone with you."

They'd only just sat down when a waiter brought them champagne. Steve was the most charming of the three, and the funniest. Seeing that he made Victoria laugh, he exaggerated his flamboyant side. He took a rose from the bouquet on the table. He admired the flower thoughfully, as if were going to offer it to Victoria, then, to the great astonishment of his friends, he picked two or three petals, dipped them in his champagne, and ate them!

"I adore rose petals in champagne. They're delicious!"

Victoria's eyes widened and she couldn't help

grimacing.

"I assure you they're good! They even make jams from them. Have you ever tried them?"

"Yes, the jams are delicious, but those are fresh roses..."

"Me, I adore them. You should try!"

"No, thank you"

"You're making a mistake. Look, you eat them like an artichoke," he said, taking some more petals.

Bernard and Chris were apparently furious about the effect Steve was having on Victoria. He amused her and made her laugh with his clowning.

"That routine with the rose petals, no one's ever tried that before with me," she murmured to Bernard with a big smile.

He was pale with jealousy, and discreetly pushed the flower decoration back towards Steve, who was busy talking to Chris.

"He's starting to annoy me, this playboy! I would like to make him swallow all these roses so that he poisons himself!" he hissed between his teeth.

Victoria burst out laughing. Was Bernard becoming jealous? That would beat everything!

"The rose petals are an antidote to alcohol. You should eat some," Steve declared perfidiously, turning towards a flabbergasted Bernard. "You've drunk a little too much tonight."

And blam! Being a good sport, Bernard smiled. Chris invited Victoria to dance. Pressing her to him, he confessed:

"Did you know you were my first love? I've never forgotten you. Through all my later girlfriends, it was really you I was looking for... Seeing you this evening was a shock. You are the woman of my life, the one in my dreams..." he said, holding her tighter.

"You, too, were my first love. We were so young! Now you live between New York and Los Angeles, me in Paris. That's life."

"How is it, beautiful as you are, that you're alone, on a day like today?"

He felt Victoria stiffen. He'd just committed a gaffe!

"I was engaged, but I broke it off. He was cheating on me."

"Then he didn't deserve you! I noticed that you're still ravaging the hearts of men as much as ever. Do you know what my friends used to call you? The "pyromaniac"!"

"The pyromaniac? Why that nickname? I don't understand."

"You seduce, you inflame, and you run. It's a little bit true, don't you think?"

"It's absolutely false!" she responded, feeling hurt.

"Don't get mad, it's a compliment. It means you're not an easy girl. You're elusive. We men think we've seduced you and then you slip through our fingers."

The music stopped, before starting again with a more languorous tune... Victoria escaped from his arms.

"Let's rejoin our friends."

"You see, I'm right!" he said, his face darkening.

Victoria didn't listen to him. She found Bernard and Steve again, in discussion with three ravishing creatures. Victoria approached the table.

"You're in excellent company, I see, so I'm leaving you. The friends I came with must be worried about my absence."

"Stay with us!" Steve and Bernard cried in chorus.

They rose to surround her with their attentions, turning

their backs on the three young girls. Offended, they disappeared.

"I made them flee! I'm sorry," she apologized, embarrassed. "Go find them..."

"Girls like that are a dime a dozen. While you are a jewel, unfortunately for us."

"That's not a nice thing to say about them!" she replied, upset.

"But it's the truth. You are beautiful and sensual. One wants to surpass oneself in order to please you. Those girls give themselves away in one night, without one having to even make an effort. Where's the romance in that?" said Steve.

"You, the playboy, are romantic?" intervened Bernard mockingly.

"Absolutely! I detest easy women, it ruins the pleasure."

"For once, I'm entirely in agreement with you!" replied Bernard.

Those young girls were cute. And just look how these machos treated them!

If a man loves you, it's he who should row towards you! Not you! It's their role to take the initiatives, they adore that. That way, they'll respect you. The wan has an infallible, formidable arm which very few men can resist: their femininity. While playing the card of docility, they obtain everything through their intelligence, their powers of seduction, and their intuition. Very few of you use them. But you'll lose out if you try to assert yourselves and become the equal of the man. That was what Madame Liouba told girls in Eastern Europe, Tatiana has told her.

Seeing her friends behave this way with women, Victoria was obliged to admit that this Madame Liouba didn't have things completely wrong!

Surrounded by these three handsome young men who courted her, Victoria felt like a flower in bloom. She wanted to forget for just one night the poisoned arrow that Cupid had planted in her heart, paralyzing her for life. She knew this in the deepest part of herself: it was the reason why she remained indifferent to the men trying to win her affections. She would like so much for a miracle from God. To forget, to forget all about him... But he lived in all the pores of her skin...

Chris came over to sit on her right, profiting from the fact that Bernard had gotten up to look for some tidbits. Steve was on her left. Stuck between the two me, she couldn't escape. All of a sudden, Victoria felt through her dress Steve's hand place itself on her knee. She was about to react when a second hand, that of Chris, came to caress the first. The two men were caressing one another's hands!

They immediately realized their mistake and promptly withdrew their hand, blush at the ridiculousness of the situation. In order not to burst out in a fit of giggles, Victoria preferred to slip away and invented an excuse. She found Maya and told her this anecdote. It had been a long time since she had laughed so hard! When she came back, Chris wouldn't leave her for a second, Steve continued to court her, and Bernard sulked. Victoria had found her smile again!

The party ended in the early hours of the morning. It was in fact nearly 5 a.m. She learned that all three men had gone to Miami before coming to Palm Beach. They were returning to New York that very same day in the private plane belonging to Steve's father.

"Come with us to New York," Chris insisted.

"No, I can't do that to my friends. Anyways, I'm returning to Paris in two days' time."

Once he was back in New York, Bernard spent his nights in clubs trying to forget Victoria. He was in love with her to the point of going mad. Sitting at the bar of a fashionable club, he was working on his sixth glass of whiskey, his mind beginning to fog over, when he felt a hand place itself on his shoulder...
"Well! What a surprise!"
Bernard turned round, and to his great amazement, recognized Alex.
"I thought you were in Singapore?"
"I came to New York on business and took advantage of the fact to spend the holidays here."
In order to talk in peace, they moved to a table. Alex spoke of his work, and asked Bernard questions about his projects. Bernard noticed that he had changed, that he was no longer the same. His face was drawn, and looked anxious, preoccupied. Bernard refrained from asking him any indiscreet questions. In any case, it was none of his business, their story was over. In contrast, Alex was more curious:
"Say, you look down. Are you having problems at work?
"No, on that side of things, everything's fine."
"In love, then?"
"Yes..."
"From the face you're making, it looks like you haven't been successful! What's he like?"
"She's the most beautiful and the most wonderful girl in the world.
"Ah!... So you've converted, too, have you?"

"Why me, too?"

"Because I'm in the same state as you."

"You mean to say...?"

Bernard burst out laughing.

"It's not funny!" Alex shot back.

"I know. But it's curious that we're both in love with a woman... You don't look too happy about it, either."

"It's an impossible love," Alex replied.

"Nothing's impossible."

"It's too complicated."

"Ah..."

"And you, what's your problem?" asked Alex.

"She's in love with another man. This happened to me when I was least expecting it."

"You're not the only one. It's strange, what's happened to us, with a woman, moreover! Let's have another drink to our health. And Happy New Year!" Alex shouted, laughing nervously.

The glasses began to line up on the table.

"It hurts so much I could die from it, this love sickness," resumed Bernard.

"You're telling me! It's unbearable, worse than torture!" Alex replied, between two hiccups. "People with serious physical injuries, when they suffer, are given morphine to ease the pain. All we have is alcohol!"

Bernard, having drunk too much, went to the toilets. When he came back, he was feeling a little better.

"Who is this girl who put you in this state?" asked Alex. "Does she live in New York?"

"No, Paris."

"They're all bitches."

"Not her."

"All of them, I tell you!" said Alex, pounding on the

table and raising his voice in his drunkenness.

Bernard could not help himself from exclaiming:

"Not your sister!"

Alex's eyes widened.

"What does my sister have to do with this conversation?"

His lips trembled and his face was livid. Had Bernard guessed his secret?

"I'm in love with Victoria," Bernard confessed.

"What? What did you say? What are you telling me? You don't know my sister!"

Bernard, seeing his sudden fury, did not answer – which only triggered more anger in Alex. He got up, took Bernard by the neck, obliging him to stand up, and delivered a blow of his fist right in the middle of the face. Bernard tried to grapple with him, but Alex continued to hit him, splitting his lower lip. Blood dripped down Bernard's chin.

"You bastard, if you touch my sister, I'll strangle you with my own two hands."

Two bouncers from the night club intervened to separate them.

"Go settle your problems outside! We don't want any trouble here!" said one of them.

It was snowing; Alex tripped, slipping with all his weight onto the pavement. Seeing him in this pitiable state, Bernard leaned towards him.

"I swear to you that nothing happened between us. Your sister is not aware of my feelings for her. She's in love with someone, she doesn't even look at me. Believe me, Alex," said Bernard, with a lump in his throat.

Alex looked at him bizarrely. In his state, he realized how absurd his actions were. Had the icy cold lashing his face returned him to his senses? Bernard seemed sincere.

"Help me stand up!" he groaned.

Bernard complied. With his handkerchief, he sponged up the blood running from his lip. He hailed a taxi.

"Where do I drop you off?"

Alex told him the address. He was bothered at losing control like that. It was the first time that had happened to him. He ended by apologizing and asking for news of Victoria. During the taxi journey, Bernard revealed the whole story to him. Perhaps as a sort of revenge towards him. He told him about the first meeting with his sister, and the suicide attempt.

"She's in Palm Beach, with friends. I saw her at the New Year's party, at Mar Largo."

Alex listened carefully, his hard pounding hard in his chest.

"How is she? I mean: from an emotional point of view?"

"Melancholy, distant... She told me one incredible thing. I don't know if she was serious, or if it was just idle talk."

"What did she say?" asked Alex, worried.

"She told that she could no longer bear material life, that her way led elsewhere, and that she wanted to take the veil! Enter a convent!

"My word, she's gone crazy. She, in a convent! I'm dreaming! She must have told you that as a joke."

"She didn't seem like she was joking. I was even surprised. But perhaps you're right: she said that when she was feeling down. One doesn't enter a convent due to a broken heart."

Alex knew Victoria well, that she was capable of carrying out her decisions to the hilt. He hoped that this idea was only a passing fancy.

"I'm going to call her in Palm Beach."

"She must be on the plane right now. She was supposed to return this evening to Paris. I wonder who the monster is who put her in this state! He can't be normal, to pass up such a jewel! Perhaps he's gay?"

Alex lowered his head, as if he'd just received a dagger blow straight to the heart. Bernard's revelations had made him come back to his senses. The taxi stopped, Alex had arrived at his destination. He got out of the car, had second thoughts, opened the door again and handed Bernard his visiting card.

"Take care of her. We'll talk on the phone. *Ciao!* And sorry for having messed you up. I'm the king of assholes!"

Bernard didn't reply. He watched thoughtfully as Alex moved off, staggering slightly.

The retreat

Upon returning to Paris, Victoria resumed her activities. Her days off were spent on retreats in various monasteries, notably in the French capital. The participants disposed of an oratory (presence of the holy sacrament), of a small library, and a garden. They were autonomous, preparing their own meals, while respecting the silence of the others. They were free to take part in the liturgy of the monastery. They could be accompanied by a nun. Some time after having gone on these rewarding retreats, Victoria asked for an appointment in order to review her spiritual and moral state with the prioress of a convent. The latter agreed to receive her and gave her accord for a retreat lasting fifteen days. The voice of the prioress sounded sweet and pleasant. What a difference from the fanatic intransigence of the mother superior in Montmartre!

When she arrived in front of the nunnery, her heart was beating wildly. Tatiana, who she'd taken into her confidence, had insisted on accompanying her.

"It's there. I've arrived."

Tatiana looked worriedly at the convent's gates. The silence behind the high wall was oppressive, even the singing of birds seemed sinister to her.

"Before you shut yourself away for a few days in this squalid place, why don't you come with me for a hot chocolate in the village café?"

Victoria hesitated. Tatiana had touched her weak point. Hot chocolate, like mashed potatoes, was a link to her early childhood. When she was sick, her mother authorized her to stay in bed during the day. It was a great pleasure, an honor. She gave her daughter family albums to look through. For the afternoon snack she prepared the best chocolate in the world, very thick, with homemade *madeleines*. And later she brought, for Victoria's dinner in bed, her favorite dish: ham and mashed potatoes. To give the burning hot potatoes time to cool down, she would trace furrows in them with the help of a fork...

"You're right, it's a good stimulant."

When they entered the café, La Mère Michel, conversation stopped. The customers, red-cheeked peasants for the most part, leaning on the bar in front of their little glasses of white wine or their coffee, stared at them in astonishment. It was nine o'clock in the morning. They sat a table, and the owner came over to take the order.

"What can I serve you?

"Could we have hot chocolate?"

"Hot chocolate? That is... I don't have..."

"But me, I have what is needed!" shouted a lady behind the counter. "I often make it for the children."

Seeing her husband's dumbfounded face, she announced:

"I'll make it for you in the kitchen."

"Why the kitchen?" her husband asked, surprised.

"Why? Because I prepare it in a saucepan!" she said, shrugging her shoulders.

"Do you want sandwiches? I just made them," the husband added.

"Sandwiches with chocolate! You must be joking! Especially since they're made with camembert!"

She addressed Tatiana and Victoria:

"Excuse him, we're in the middle of the country here, as you can see. I've prepared some *madeleines* for my children, if you'd like some."

"Oh, I adore them. How nice!" Victoria exclaimed. "Thank you, *madame*."

Victoria's eyes shone with joy. Tatiana couldn't help from saying to her:

"If I'd known you like chocolate and *madeleines* so much, I would have prepared them for you at my house."

"It's not the same thing. You can't understand. Here, it's rare to find them, and it's all the more moving. That's what makes the difference."

The owner's wife proudly carried in two big bowls. She poured hot, appetizing chocolate into them.

"Instead of standing there looking at me, go fetch the *madeleines* that are on the kitchen table," she ordered her husband.

He came back a few seconds later and put a plate filled with *madeleines* on the table.

"I think you'll like them!" the proprietress declared proudly. "It's my grandmother's recipe!"

Victoria was very touched. The two bowls and the plate were part the owners' personal dishware – which added to the value of this handsome, unexpected gesture. Like two kids, their lips covered in chocolate, they greedily ate the delights of the "*Mère Michel*" beneath the tender gaze of the other customers. The proprietress had left a napkin folded in four on the table, as a resting-place for the steaming saucepan of chocolate. This breakfast was the best in the world for Victoria, because it had been prepared with much simplicity and love. When it came time to pay the bill, Mother Michel intervened:

"It's on the house!"

Victoria insisted, embarrassed.

"It's out of the question, it gave me pleasure. This way, you'll keep a good memory of the village and of the Mère Michel café."

Victoria approached her.

"Will you permit me?"

She gave her a kiss on both cheeks. Tatiana did the same. Mother Michel was pink with happiness.

"When you pass by our place again, don't forget to come say hello."

Back in the car, silence installed itself. In the distance, a rooster's crow resounded over the landscape.

"There's a farm not far from here," Tatiana observed. "It reminds me of my village and my home. Don't you want to have a look at the farm? I'll bring back some fresh eggs and cheese..."

"Tatiana, you're forgetting the reason for my visit here. I'm not here as a tourist! Take me to the convent, then you can go look for your eggs..."

"Good fresh eggs, with orange yolks inside... Like at home," she said pensively.

"Don't forget the beet soup..."

"You're being mean."

"No, I'm teasing you."

"Are you sure you really want to go bury yourself for a few days? All this for a boor who's made you blow a fuse! You should go see a psychologist rather than the good sisters."

"You know, the prioress in Montmartre advised the same thing to me on the telephone. I had the audacity to call her again to provoke her. When she heard my voice,

I thought she was going to choke. She told me that she would formally oppose my joining her community. I answered her insolently: 'May God forgive your meanness and your dry heart, my mother!" I hung up without waiting for her reaction."

"Decidedly, I'm unable to understand you. You have everything going for you and you're going to lose it all on a mad impulse. If Bernard calls to find out how you're doing, what should I tell him?"

"That I've gone away on a trip for a few days."

"You'll phone to keep me informed?"

"That's right, we'll even communicate by e-mail... And Sunday, you'll bring me cakes and vodka..."

"You'd like that?"

"Not at all. I'm joking. I'm going to be cut off here from the world for several days. It's a world of prayer and meditation. This can only do me good. Go on with you, goodbye, Tatiana. Don't say anything to anybody. I'm counting on you."

"You know I won't. I need some advice from you. What should I do about Bernard? Can I confess to him that I'm in love?"

"Have you lost your mind? In your place, I wouldn't make a move, I would forget about him, even. You're married. Face the truth. Don't give up the prey for the shadow, you'll have nothing to show for it in the end. I would like you to avoid suffering. But you won't listen to me, I know. Go on, goodbye."

Tatiana saw Victoria ring the bell at the gate. She took off at full spend, making the tires squeal, as if the Devil was pursuing her.

The nun who received her was radiant. She asked if Victoria had had a good journey. Apparently, she was neither unhappy nor sullen. *It's a good sign*, Victoria thought. This welcome comforted her. She went with the nun to drop off her things. Judging by a documentary she'd seen about a model prison in the United States, that was a palace compared to her tiny cell! It was furnished with a mattress set on a trestle, a chair, and a small sink...

"I'll take you to the office of the mother superior."

The prioress was waiting for her with a benevolent smile. Fairly round in corpulence, her ageless face still kept the bloom of her beauty. Was it perhaps the reflection of a serenity and a great goodness that gave her this charisma? She was nothing like the prioress in Montmartre! She asked Victoria about the motives for her decision, trying with considerable diplomacy to dissuade her. But Victoria expressed her determination. The mother superior listened to her with attention, her gaze betraying the emotion that this young girl instilled in her. She reminded her of the striking image of her own younger sister, called to God at the age of twenty. Was it a sign from Heaven? She had a lump in her throat and her eyes began to sting. Victoria had the same voice, the same look, and the same body language. The emotion was poignant, especially since today would have been her sister's birthday.

Victoria's intuition told her that she'd found an ally. The mother superior shortened the interview with delicacy, out of fear of betraying her weakness. She advised the girl to stay for fifteen days in order to participate and share her faith with the other nuns, living at the community's rhythm.

During her stay, she prayed, meditated, and sang with the nuns. She participated in the recreational moments as well the hard chores. The more the days went by, the more the prioress was convinced that Victoria was worthy of joining them, if she so desired.

Valentine's Day

Television, radio, the magazines, and the store windows all declared with great pomp the feast-day of lovers: Saint Valentine's Day. Red hearts, in paper, or in chocolate... inundated Paris! It was impossible to miss seeing them! Even all the fruit and vegetable vendors displayed the red heart. At the butchers', there were heart-shaped blood sausages; the delicatessens had hearts of cold meats; and at the bakers' it was the bread! As for the programs on television it was even worse: romances, kisses, songs, couples displaying their love for one another...

To be sure, it was beautiful, but it was unbearable for Victoria. On the day in question, she remained shut up at home with the telephone unplugged. She spent the entire day in bed under her duvet, crying her eyes out, while nibbling chocolates and little cakes, offering herself two or three glasses of champagne to bandage her heart's wounds. It was the most horrible day of the year for solitary hearts. This celebration only increased the pain of singles and outcasts. There must be great numbers of people who, like her, hated this day!

The turning point

Several months had gone by... when Victoria at last received her admission to the convent. It caused general stupefaction around her. Her friends tried to dissuade her, but there was no changing her mind. Since Alex had left, she'd been through an ordeal. His brother no longer sent his news. Nothing more attached her to this life, nothing that interested her. Nothing, except Alex and this love that ate at her, that smothered her day and night. Only this form of exile could kill the poison circulating in her veins, by forgetting everything and giving herself to God for the rest of her days.

Bernard learned of the news from Tatiana. Since his return from New York, he had tried to contact her, but in vain. Victoria had become inaccessible. Her answering machine tirelessly announced that she was traveling...

Tatiana was there in case of need. As for Fiona, she had left to live in London with her new boyfriend; they were soon to marry. She had finally forgotten her handsome Italian who'd been making her suffer. Victoria was happy for her. Tatiana, by dint of patience, managed to sleep with Bernard. Unfortunately, not only did this experience end in failure, but she also received a mighty slap in the face. Bernard no longer wanted anything to do with her, despite her supplications and inflamed declarations of love! She then confided in Victoria, who boosted her morale and finally revealed, to ease Tatiana's sorrow and salvage her pride, that she'd heard it said that Bernard was a homosexual. Tatiana had trouble believing this, of course. But the world is small, and she received confirmation from other friends. It hurt her very badly and she was disappointed, but this revelation and the attitude he'd displayed towards her had the effect of provoking a veritable rejection of him. So everything went back to normal.

"I never would have imagined that so virile a man could be a homosexual!"

"Virility has nothing to do with it. It's how things are in life. So, now you know that you didn't lose anything. He doesn't like women. You have a marvelous husband, keep him. The real men, in our times, are hard to come by, they don't grow on trees... You're lucky to have found a man who loves you. Keep him, make him happy and produce beautiful children for him. That's all he's waiting for."

Sister Marie-Ange

Victoria had difficulties getting used to her new life. She had wanted to punish herself for a mortal sin, and she couldn't have found a better form of chastisement: scrubbing, waxing, sweeping, ironing, tidying, gardening, cooking, and praying without respite, in an endless cycle. Without comfort and without heating. It was forbidden to communicate with another sister about personal problems. Victoria accepted this new descent into hell with courage and philosophy. Nevertheless, this wouldn't last: she knew herself, she hated injustice, treachery, and hypocrisy, so it was not long before her nature asserted itself. One morning when she was feeling fed up, when she realized that her youth would perish in a gloomy ambience, she disturbed the community with pranks as only she was capable of inventing. She hid the homespun dress of one sister while she was sleeping, because she was giving Victoria a hard time, and stole the cornet of another nun... The complaints against her accumulated, and a petition circulated. Since her arrival in the convent, Victoria had been sowing the seeds of rebellion. She couldn't help herself. She wanted to dust off all this hypocrisy, inn order to favor the love of God and her fellow human beings. She thought that she would find in places such as these respect for others, serenity, wisdom of the spirit, generosity of heart, and goodness in general. Not at all! Most of the nuns were hypocritical old cows! The mother superior was disappointed, she tried to temper the behavior of her protégée; she closed her eyes to a lot of things, each time finding excuses. Victoria had the same character as her late sister, Danielle! She was obliged, for the example, to convoke her. She was very angry with her, giving her a warning. Victoria, using her charm, denied everything. She said that she was the scapegoat of jealous and unscrupulous sisters. Nevertheless, before the scale of this intolerable situation, the mother superior sought out monsignor the bishop, to ask him for counsel and to pacify the hatred that taken hold of the convent since Victoria had arrived. Visits from the outside world took place once a month. Tatiana, passing herself off as Victoria's cousin, obtained the right to come see her. Victoria found a way to telephone her in secret, placing orders with her for vodka and caviar... It was easy for Tatiana, with friends coming regularly from her country to procure these very onerous products cheaply. Victoria had a plan. Monsignor the bishop was supposed to visit the convent, in order to resolve the problem of all these complaints against her.

Victoria, who had become "Sister Marie-Ange", was on kitchen duty that day, as usual. The lunch started. To the bishop's great surprise, Sister Marie-Ange, addressed him while serving the pastry she had prepared.

"Monsignor, if you permit me, I'm going to serve you a glass of vodka, ordered especially for you. For pastry with caviar, you can't say no to that," she said in her most charming manner. "It's my cousin who brought all this in your honor."

An angel fallen from heaven!, the bishop, who was a *bon viveur*, thought to himself. He'd been apprehensive of this lunch for several days now.

The prioress almost choked: Sister Marie-Ange was

aggravating her case. She wanted to intervene, but the bishop preempted her:

"Excellent idea," he said, surprised. "Pastry with caviar, and vodka! What a feast!"

Sister Marie-Ange took care to copiously soak the pastry in vodka, knowing that caviar induced thirst. She even poured a little in the water pitchers... The result was not long in manifesting itself. The tone rose at the table, and laughter burst forth. The good sisters were entitled, they too, to a few grains of pleasure, obviously far less so than the monsignor and the prioress. But a good-sized glassful of vodka mixed in with the caviar sauce perfumed each plate. They were laughing and cooing out loud. The chocolate cakes were filled with an aphrodisiac, a "Tatiana" specialty, for which Sister Marie-Ange was unable to obtain the secret. She had merely been ordered to add in this mixture during the preparation? The result exceeded all her hopes... To the point that she panicked and began to feel guilty. To calm them, she made mocha coffee, with an aftertaste of chocolate, that she had also ordered from her accomplice, Tatiana. But instead of attenuating the madness that had seized the convent, it only stirred up the ambiance further. For the sisters, it was a party: at the bottom of their hearts they blessed Sister Marie-Ange for putting a little spice into this place of sadness. Without her, they couldn't never have imagined such a feast, in such an atmosphere. One nun, a bit tipsy, began to dance a Viennese waltz, sweeping in the others along with her. The bishop was beside himself with joy. It was hilarious when viewed from the outside, but it no longer made Sister Marie-Ange laugh. She left the room, a little frightened, and headed for the prioress's office to call Tatiana, hoping that she would be at home.

"Hello?"

"Tatiana, it's me, Sister Mar... I mean to say: Victoria. Tatiana, it's awful, I did just what you told me, but it's become madness. The whole convent, except for me, is rolling under the table – in a manner of speaking. They're singing, and dancing! I hope they're not going to dance the French cancan or take to striptease! Help me! What should I do!"

"Wait for it to pass. No one will suspect that you did it on purpose. Don't worry. As for the bishop, he'll have experienced an unforgettable moment. I don't think after this that you'll be receiving a convocation from the diocese. That's great! Super!"

Tatiana had a fit of giggles.

"Well, I have to leave you. I'll be in more trouble if they find me here."

"Judging by what you described to me, I'd be surprised if the mother superior can get around very easily right now!"

"Even so, it's not the vodka that's put them in such a state. What is it, that mixture you gave me? Is it dangerous?"

"Not at all! Don't worry. Thanks to you, they will enjoy a few hours in paradise... Go on! *Ciao!* Kisses," she said, bursting with laughter.

The party atmosphere have reached a climax. Monsignor was asking for more vodka.

"I'm sorry, monsignor, the bottle is empty," said Sister Marie-Ange.

"No, no," intervened Sister Marie-Madeleine, "there's still a whole bottle in the kitchen!"

Well, if Sister Marie-Madeleine is joining in, too...

"I have for Monsignor a brandy that's twenty years old!" the prioress proudly announced.

It would beat everything if the prioress also offered him a cigar... Say, she should have thought of that herself...

"Twenty years old! I can't refuse this elixir!" he said, with his cheeks red, a smile on his lips, and his eyes bulging.

Here they go again! Victoria returned to the kitchen to put things in order a bit. Sister Cécile wanted to help her clear the tables, but she was staggering. Victoria went to look for help from a sister who was in bed with a severe case of bronchitis. She explained the situation, without of course giving the true version. This sister could serve as a witness in case of any kind of repercussions...

"I'm feeling much better. I'll come help you," she said, all excited.

Discovering the spectacle, the eyes and mouth of Sister Marie-Joseph grew curiously round.

"But what happened to them?" she asked, completely dumbfounded, her arms dangling at her sides.

Seeing her expression, Victoria had difficulty stopping herself from giggling.

"They haven't properly digested my pastry with caviar," she said jestingly.

"Pastry with caviar? I've never eaten that in my whole life! Is there any left?"

"No, no, there's none left. Go clear the tables."

As soon as the other sister turned her back, Victoria regretfully threw away the rest of the pastry, but she forgot the cakes on the tables: Sister Marie-Josèphe could not resist the sin of greed...

For a whole week, the sisters would be doing penance...

No one spoke any more of complaints against Sister Marie-Ange.

Love beneath the veil

Since the famous lunch which would remain memorable for the entire community, the attitude of the nuns changed with respect to Sister Marie-Ange. They were nice to her, ad even admired her. But Sister Marie-Ange suddenly calmed down – a development that worried the prioress. Her expression became elusive and distracted. She almost would have preferred her being mischievous. During her moments of relaxation, Sister Marie-Ange went to pray in the chapel, her heart heavy with tears. She carried the original sin within herself, her nights were still visited by Lucifer who infused her with carnal desires. Alex inhabited her dreams...

But one day, her face lit up, radiant with joy at the news of an unforeseen visit.

"Sister Marie-Ange, you are awaited in the visitors' room," announced Sister Cécile.

"But it's not visiting day!"

"It's your brother who's arrived from abroad to see you. The prioress has given him special permission."

Sister Marie-Ange turned pale. She felt herself wobbling under the shock of this unexpected visit. Sister Cécile helped her sit down.

"It's the emotion, it's normal," said Sister Cécile.

Sister Marie-Ange passed her hand across her forehead, gathering her wits about her.

"I don't want to receive him!"

"But you don't really think that! It's not right, he's come all that way just for you!"

"All right, I'll be there in a few minutes, have him wait."

In the visitors' room, for a few minutes that seemed interminable, Alex paced back and forth to quiet his nerves. His heart was pounding hard, he had a lump in his throat, and his hands were freezing. He heard a rustle, then a wire mesh window opened partway and the face of his sister appeared, covered by a white veil. The shock was such that he gave a start despite himself. He looked at her, feeling stunned. Beneath the veil, her face was sublime with beauty. He clenched his fists. For the first time in his life, he wanted to cry. He remained standing there, as if petrified. He could not even hold her in his arms or kiss her.

"Hello, Alexandre. Why didn't you warn me of your visit?"

"I was afraid you'd refuse to see me."

There was silence on Victoria's part. Then, with a sigh:

"You were right. How are you. Your life? Your work? Your loves?"

"My life is a desert, my work is going well – on that score, I have no problems. It's you I'm worried about. Why did you do this? Spoiling your life, burying yourself alive. Since I found out, I've been going mad, I can't sleep anymore at night, I have no desire for life without you. If I became a monk and lived secluded in a monastery, or if I blew my brains away, what would be your reaction? Did you think about me?"

"It's not because of us that I took the veil. Since my childhood, I dreamed of devoting myself to God. I'm very happy here, I've found my way."

Through the little opening, she passed her hand to caress his cheek in a sign of tenderness. He held it, to place upon it a furtive kiss. To deflect the violent commotion that seized her, she talked to him about her apartment.

Since entering the convent, she had given him permission to live there, making him promise not to sell it yet.

"Don't worry, Vic, I've sold my apartment. When I come to Paris, I live at your place. I haven't touched a thing. Everything is just as you left it. You never know, one day you may change your mind, something I wish with all my heart. I've engaged an administrator to pay the bills. He takes care of our affairs when I'm not there. Henriette comes one time a week to air the place and do a little housecleaning. You see, I've thought of everything."

"That's perfect. You know, Alexandre, I would like so much to know that you were happy. I pray to God every day for you."

He opened his heart to his beloved, smashing the taboos.

"It's not prayers I need, but your presence! I can't live without you, I'm chained to you, to your skin, to your body, to your life. Victoria, my love, I love you, this love wears me down, it tears my guts out. I could never love anyone else but you. I want to take you far, far away with me, to a desert island. I will invent a new life for us."

"Shhhh! I am Sister Marie-Ange. Victoria no longer exists. Victoria is dead."

The tone was icy. Alex had the impression of receiving a hard slap to the face. A long shiver ran through him. He looked at this novice who was no more than the ghost of Victoria. The monotonous voice of Sister Marie-Ange gave him a start:

"I have to leave you now. You have my permission to write and give me your news. But you should know that the mail is opened before they pass it on to me.

Goodbye, Alex."

She called him Alex, like she used to do. She closed the window. Victoria's face retreated into the half-light and then disappeared. He heard a door close softly, very softly behind her. He drummed with rage against the wire mesh, shouting:

"Vic! Vic! Come back!"

But only a heavy silence answered him. He left the visitors' room, his face contorted with pain. His calls had reached the office of the prioress. She came towards him. She saw the tears in his eyes, and felt a pang seeing his suffering. She spoke to him in a voice full of tenderness:

"Sister Marie-Ange is happy among us. Don't perturb her, she is a fragile child."

Outside the sun shone with all its fires to celebrate the springtime, the trees were flowering, the birds sang their joy. In Alex's heart, the sky was black, it rained in his eyes, and the birdsong seemed like the prelude to a funeral. Bernard was waiting for him in the car, nervously smoking a cigarette. He got out hastily to come meet Alex.

"Already? Did you see her?"

"Yes..."

"How is she?"

"It's not her. It's her ghost..."

"Her ghost? What do you mean?"

"Come on, let's get out of here before I do something stupid!"

During the journey that brought them back to Paris, Alex did not say a word, his jaw clenched shut. Bernard respected his friend's emotion. He himself was not feeling much at ease. He was still in love with Victoria, he hadn't managed to forget her. Alex spoke no more of their fight in New York. It was as if he took no account of that shameful night.

Alexandre had arrived that morning from Singapore. He dropped his bags at Victoria's, took a shower, then phoned Bernard to ask if he was willing to accompany him to see his sister. Bernard had not hesitated, he cancelled his meetings to go with him. For Victoria, he would have gone to the end of the world. Unfortunately, he had not foreseen that he would be forbidden access to her. But imagining her behind those walls twisted his heart.

"If only you had seen her! Despite the white veil that concealed her hair, her beauty was almost supernatural. I had trouble meeting her eyes. Her lips trembled... I'm going mad! Now I have to go to her apartment, where her presence is constant. I haven't touched anything, it's all as it was. I'm going to find her in the odor of her perfume, in her clothing, in her personal objects. I'm going mad!" he repeated. "No one can understand me."

He punched his forehead to signal his rage. Bernard had shivers running through his body. Alex was speaking of his sister like a lover! All of a sudden, he felt a malaise coming over him. It was an unhealthy situation. A thought crossed his mind, but he quickly chased it away, ashamed that it could even have occurred to him. But all the same, that crisis in New York, and Victoria suddenly taking the veil, after a failed suicide attempt... That passion she had when she spoke of her brother, who was her god... Could they be in love with one another, to the point of this extremity? If that was their secret truth, it was horrible. But no, it wasn't possible, the love he felt for Victoria was making him delirious. Alex's voice interrupted his thoughts:

"I'm going to bring Victoria's affairs up to date, see her accountant and the bank, then I'm returning to Singapore. I should stay a few days longer, but I don't see the interest now, after the shock I just received."

"I understand..."

"Tell me, do you still have your motorcycle?"

"Yes, of course. Why? Do you need it?"

"Yes, it seems a nuisance to rent a car for only four days. And parking in Paris is always a hassle! With this fine weather, the bike would be more pleasant."

"No problem, if you want, you can take it now."

"I knew I could count on you."

Alex recovered the motorcycle from Bernard's garage.

"I'll call you so that we can go get a meal together before I leave," Alex said, before shooting off on the bike.

Bernard watched him go. He shook his head. For him, his friend's attitude spelled trouble. But fortunately, Alex was going back to Singapore; with time, things would fall back into place...

Alex stopped at his sister's bank. He had a power of attorney, allowing him to deal with her business concerns. Everything was in order, her money was being well-managed. Normally, when one enters a convent, one gives up all one's worldly goods to the community. But Victoria, prudent, had kept hers, because, if she changed her mind in the course of the year, she would find herself in difficulty. Alex phoned the accountant:

"I'm in Paris for four days. Can you give me an appointment?"

"When can you drop by? If you're not far from my

office, I can see you in a half hour. A client cancelled on me."

"I'm on my way. See you then."

Alex discussed several matters with him. The man knew of Victoria's situation, but did not comment on her decision to enter a convent. He called his secretary and asked to bring the personal letters addressed to Victoria. "I threw away the junk mail and opened the business letters, as we agreed. But this mail is personal, so I put it aside. Here's all there is."

Alexandre thanked him, leaving the office feeling reassured. On that side, everything was fine. In any case, he could communicate with the accountant by fax or e-mail if a problem arose. He arrived at the apartment, where he glanced through the letters. He even took the initiative of opening them. There was nothing of interest. He casually looked at a hand-addressed envelope, which bore the stamp of an antique dealer. It must be an invitation or an ad. He opened it. The dealer mentioned that he was safekeeping for his sister a document that had been forgotten in a writing desk. Alexandre gave a start. He read the message two or three times. Then, without any hesitation, he telephoned. The dealer confirmed his missive. Alex went to the store in question. A man who was past his prime received him. At his questioning expression, Alex was certain that he knew the contents of the document that he'd found. He asked for proof of Alex's identity. Then he opened a drawer, pulled out a beige envelope, and handed it to Alex, saying in a quavering voice:

"I sold the writing desk a year ago, maybe longer. No matter. The client who bought it discovered this letter. He brought it to me so that I could restitute it to the seller. I slipped it into this envelope. As I note down everything in my policy ledger, I found your address. So, there you have it."

Alexandre thanked him and left the antique shop, without giving a glance to the marvels on display. He was in a hurry to open the letter. There was a bar just opposite; he took the opportunity to go have a coffee. The envelope was burning his fingers. He unsealed it. Inside, there was another beige envelope, stamped, with his mother's name and address, that had been opened. His mother had died two years ago, already! Why had she hidden this letter? What would he discover? A secret liaison? His vision blurred. He opened the envelope and took out the letter to read it, his face marked by astonishment. The author, a woman, asked his mother to contact her: she had important revelations to communicate to her. She provided her address and telephone number.

Without a moment's hesitation, he decided to call her on his cell phone. A feminine voice answered:

"Hello?"

"*Bonjour, madame.* Are you Madame Violine?"

"Yes."

Alexandre explained the object of his call.

"Your *maman* told you nothing about this?"

"No, she died."

There was a moment of silence on the other end. Then:

"How long ago?"

Alexandre informed her of the date and year of his mother's death. The woman replied:

"Can you excuse me a minute?"

"By all means," he answered, surprised, "take your time."

A few minutes went by and Alex began to grow impatient.

"Here we are, I found it. What was the cause of her passing?"

"An automobile accident. She died instantly."

"My God! That's terrible!"

"What is it? What are you hiding from me?"

"I can't tell you anything. Goodbye, *monsieur*.

Then she hung up brusquely. Alex, stupefied, tried her number again. In vain. She would no longer answer. She even took her phone off the hook. Perplexed, Alexandre ordered a sandwich and a glass of wine. It was 3:30 p.m. and he hadn't eaten lunch yet. All these emotions made his head swim. He needed to think things over. With the jet lag, his mind was muddled. Why did the woman become so panicked? He paid the bill, climbed back onto the motorcycle and headed off in the direction of the direction of the village where she lived, near the city of Dreux, west of Paris. He stopped at a florist's. After asking for directions, he found without too much difficulty the detached house belonging to this Madame Violine. When he rang the bell at the garden gate, two dogs, a German shepherd a setter, rushed up, barking at him through the fence and baring their teeth.

"Be quiet! Calm down!" a voice shouted.

A woman emerged onto the front porch of the house. She was medium in height, and fairly stout, with short, blonde hair and a pleasant, smiling face. Her age must have been about sixty. She looked at Alexandre inquisitively.

"Who are you looking for, *monsieur*?

"Madame Violine."

"That's me."

Madame Violine was impressed by this big, handsome, stylish fellow. Alex took the bouquet of flowers from his saddlebag.

"I apologize for insisting. It's me who called you a short while ago. I have to speak with you, it's important. I've come from abroad; could you see me for a few minutes? I won't keep you long," he implored her gently.

Seeing the distress in his eyes, the lady opened the gate. Alexandre handed her the bouquet. His delicate gesture touched her deeply. It had been a long time since she'd received flowers! Except for the roses from her own garden...

"You shouldn't have..." she said, smelling the flowers.

She bade him to enter her living room, which was warm and prettily arranged.

"Would you like a cup of tea or coffee?"

"Nothing, thank you. I want only to hear you, to learn the motive behind this letter."

Madame Violine sat down facing him. She looked at him with a troubled expression, seeking the right words.

"Is it so serious as that?" Alexandre asked, worried. While coming here, I realized that my mother's accident took place nearby. Had she learned something from you that would have upset her? I have to know."

Madame Violine's hands shook and her face became livid. She hesitated, but couldn't avoid the truth any longer:

"Prepare yourself for a shock. What I have to say concerns you in particular. I've kept this heavy secret for long years now. It's prevented me many times from getting to sleep. A little over two years ago, I was serious ill, I underwent an operation on my heart. Overcome with panic at the idea of taking this secret to my grave, I wrote to your mother, hoping she hadn't moved. I had telephoned the municipality previously. Your *maman* came and I revealed everything to her. She left my home distressed. I was a little frightened at the idea of her driving in such a state. But she replied that she would be fine. That she let me know regarding her decision. After that, I never heard from her again... One thing I know is that she forgave me, and even better: she kissed me and thanked me for the beautiful gift that I had offered her. She held me in her arms, she was in tears. I asked her, 'You don't hate me?' And she said, 'On the contrary, I bless you, just as I thanked God that day for the beautiful baby that Hr had given me!'"

Alexander felt anxiety starting to take hold of him. Madame Violine was frightened of getting to the point. He didn't dare interrupt her, fearing that she would change her mind about telling him. Her eyes lost in the past, evading his gaze, Madame Violine started her tale:

It's me who helped your *maman* give birth. The delivery was very difficult and the baby didn't survive. In the same room, a young girl of fifteen had just died bringing a superb baby into the world. Upon her arrival at the clinic, she had told us that she did not want to keep the child, whose father had died of an overdose a few months earlier. She lacked the means to take care of it. Without any family, she had just left the public orphanage where she'd been raised. Having witnessed both these tragedies, I switched the babies. The decision took place quickly right there in my head. The live baby would have been given to an agency that dealt with cases of abandonment like this. He was so beautiful! The other parents, who awaited their child like the coming of the Messiah, were going to be crushed by the news. I believe in God, I'm a churchgoer, and I thought I was doing the right thing according to my conscience, in the face of an injustice of this sort! If I had to do it all over, I would do the same thing."

Alex had a lump in his throat, and tears he couldn't control rolled down his cheeks. He didn't know if it was shock, emotion, or his joy at not being Victoria's brother by blood. Everything became confused in his head.

"Would you like an old brandy?" Madame Violine asked timidly. "It will do you good."

"I'd like that very much. Thank you."

He took out a package of cigarettes and asked:

"May I?"

"Please do," she said, pushing forward an ashtray. "Do you hate me?"

"Not at all! On the contrary! Thanks to you, I had wonderful parents, a golden childhood, and the most beautiful love affair in the world. I'm feeling an infinite happiness, and an immense shock. I can't find words that are strong enough."

At that point, Madame Violine could no longer hold back her tears, and emotion seized her. Alexandre stood up, and she did the same:

"Will you permit me, *madame*?

Without waiting for an answer, he took her in his arms, and embraced her tightly.

"It's my turn to tell you a horrible secret. I'm madly in love with my own sister, to the point of losing my reason, and she, too. Moreover, I've been living in exile to try and forget her, while my sister has entered a convent. We've been living a true ordeal, for months now. You are our providence! Now I can love her openly, marry her, and have children! We can at last escape from this hell. You've been our fairy godmother.

Madame Violine looked at him, speechless. She couldn't get over it. It was worthy of a novel, a beautiful love story. Alex, of course, did not admit that they had been actual lovers: the good lady would have been horrified. A widow for over twenty years, she had no family and lived alone in this house, with her two dogs as her sole companions. She had never had children. She would have liked so much to have kept for herself the handsome little baby that she had helped bring into the world... That was the true explanation for her impetuous act the day he was born. With her eyes full of tears, she confessed as much to Alexandre on her doorstep.

"You will not be alone anymore, now. I will never forget what you have done for me, for us. I owe you my destiny. From now on, I'll be coming to see you, with my sister... I mean to say: Victoria and I. It's going to come as a shock to her, but I sure that she will be overcome with joy, like I am. I am going immediately to tell her the news, get her out of that convent, and take her with me to the other side of the world. A new life will begin for us. My head is full of dreams. Thank you, my God! Thank you, Madame Violine!"

He held her tightly in his arms, before climbing onto the motorcycle. Over the throbbing of the engine he called out to her:

"I'm going to find her! I'll be in touch. See you soon, and thank you!"

Madame Violine watched the motorcycle drive off. She was deeply moved, tears flowed down her face, and sobs sprang from her throat. What a story!

Alexander felt as if wings had sprouted from his back. To be sure, he'd just found out that he was an illegitimate child and that he would never know his true parents, but love was stronger than anything. He headed in the direction of the convent, he could not wait any longer to announce his news to her. He accelerated to maximum speed, as if to make up for lost time. He would hire a boat, take her to the islands. He would make her a queen and love her so strongly that the most beautiful star in the sky would turn green with jealousy. He had never been so happy in his entire life. Rain fell, fine and sticky, but for him, it was a rain of stars, and the sun shone in his heart. The motorcycle sped like a racing car towards his beloved. A truck changed lanes in front of him, without having put on its signals beforehand; Alex, surprised, tried to avoid it. Too late, he was sandwiched between the truck and the car following closely behind. The collision was violent. Stuck in the metal wreckage of his bike, Alexandre lay motionless. The automobile drivers who witnessed the accident were frantic. The truck driver descended from his vehicle, as did the man in the vehicle behind. They gaped at the damage caused through their own fault. They didn't know if he was alive or dead.

The emergency services arrived in the minutes that followed; they carefully extracted Alexander's body, which lay in a pool of blood and metal debris. He was the only injured person. Transported to the nearest hospital, the police found among his papers the name and the number of Madame Violine, as well as those of the convent. Contacted by the police, Madame Violine had a nervous attack. She screamed that they must inform his ster, who was at the convent. When the prioress received the terrible news, she told Victoria that her brother had been the victim of an accident. Victoria, distraught, begged her to call a taxi. The prioress complied immediately.

When Victoria arrived at the hospital, Alexandre was undergoing X-ray examination: his injuries were deep, and brain damage was feared. The wait was interminable. They brought him into the intensive care unit, and the doctor did not disguise his worry. Victoria asked if she could see him for a few minutes. Confronted with her homespun dress, the white veil, and her angelic face reddened by tears, the doctor granted her five minutes, but no more. Upon seeing her brother, with his entire head wrapped in bandages and an intravenous drip attached to each arm, she felt her legs start to give way. She approached the bed and leaned over his bed to kiss him. Alexandre opened his eyes, recognized Victoria, and said something she could not understand.

"Alexandre, my love, my love, can you hear me? Say something. I beg you!"

She heard him murmur:

"I love you..."

His head fell back on the pillow and his eyes closed again. Victoria panicked:

"Alexandre, my love, my beloved, I'm here, I love you!"

A nurse had just entered the room; the sight of this beautiful nun in tears leaning over the patient troubled her strangely. She heard the last words uttered by the sister. Surprised, she stood there with her mouth wide open. Her glance registered in a stupor the cardiac arrest on the heart monitor. She beeped the doctor who arrived immediately with his assistants. The nurse asked Victoria to leave the room. They made several attempts to resuscitate the body, but in vain... They could only make note of the death.

"Was he member of your family, my sister?" asked the doctor, coming to join her in the hallway.

"My brother..."

"I'm sorry, we did everything possible to save him. It's better that it happened this way for him. He would have remained paralyzed. Be brave, my sister, be brave."

Victoria cried out:

"No, it's not true, it's not possible!"

She pushed past the doctor to return to the room where her brother lay. She held him in her arms, covering his face with kisses. Madness took hold of her.

"He isn't dead! You must save him!" she sobbed. "Alex, answer me, answer me, I beg you! Don't leave me..."

Her pain, her sobbing and her cries had a lugubrious echo. The nurses, although used to such tragedies, were transfixed. Driven by compassion, they tried to console her:

"Calm yourself, my sister, calm yourself. Don't stay here. Come."

Looking lost, she left the room. She came across a lady, who was none other than Madame Violine.

"My sister, my sister, I must speak with you."

Victoria didn't see her, didn't hear her. Her eyes crazed and wild, she spoke to herself and murmured like a prayer:

"My Alex, I'm coming to join you. We won't suffer anymore, we'll be happy now."

Like a specter, she headed towards a window, swiftly opened it, leaned out, then let herself tumble into the void... It all happened so quickly, no one had time to intervene

"No, not that!"

Madame Violine's cry ripped through the silence. She toppled to the floor under her full weight: her sick heart had not resisted. It stopped, carrying away forever the secret of this love beneath the veil.

Table des matières